LEADING YOUTH MINISTRY

BY DOUG FRANKLIN

AN INTERACTIVE RESOURCE TO HELP YOUTH WORKERS GROW IN LEADERSHIP

Developing Leaders to Fulfill the Great Commission

Leading Youth Ministry
Copyright © 2011 by LeaderTreks

Published by LeaderTreks
25W560 Geneva Road, Suite 30, Carol Stream, IL 60188

Printed in the United States of America

ISBN: 978-1-934577-09-7

www.leadertreks.com
877-502-0699

Table of Contents

Leading Youth Ministry

Introduction

In ministry, one of the biggest challenges we face is the development of our own leadership abilities. So much rests on our capacity to effectively lead those who serve with us in ministry as well as the students whose lives we are trying to impact. You probably feel the weight of being a better leader every day. You know how important it is to lead your volunteer team. You recognize that your students need you to cast a compelling vision for the student ministry. We don't have to convince you of the need to grow as a leader; you already know this intrinsically. The struggle comes in knowing where to turn for practical lessons that will improve your ability to lead. That's our goal for this book.

At LeaderTreks we have been training youth pastors and students in leadership for years. We have identified many of the important skills that youth workers need to master in order to be successful leaders in their churches. The job of a youth worker is varied and complex. The position requires the tact of a politician, the motivation of a coach, and the love of a mother. Being a successful leader in this environment requires a person who is learning from every situation and willing to do the hard things it takes to be a great leader.

We are excited that you have chosen to join us on this adventure. Being a leader is a high calling, one that will require the best from you. By working through this book, it is our hope that you will be equipped and motivated to tackle the challenges that lie ahead.

A Look Inside

Leading Youth Ministry is a unique resource designed to help you become a better leader. This book will uncover leadership lessons that will easily apply to your ministry situation. You will learn about your leadership personality and how to maximize your strengths to the benefit of your ministry. This book uses the proven LeaderTreks leadership development strategy that is expressed in the equation:

Leadership Principles + Leadership Experiences = Transformational Leadership.

This formula is foundational to all that we do and it holds the key to unlocking your potential as a leader. By following this leadership blueprint you will learn key lessons that will help you become a more balanced leader.

Each chapter focuses on a relevant leadership topic. First, you will learn the leadership principle through a narrative story and a selection of scripture. These sections reemphasize the leadership principles. The chapter will then provide an activity that relates to the leadership topic and several application questions. These sections are designed to give you a specific leadership experience. Each chapter will contain the following elements:

• A narrative story – We will follow in the footsteps of a fictional youth worker as he struggles to grow as a leader. Many of the issues he faces may be very similar to some of your challenges in ministry. This section will uncover a leadership truth that you can apply in your ministry.

• A Biblical truth (leadership principle) – Next, we will take a look at an instance in the life of Jesus that reinforces the truth that has been uncovered. Christ provides a great example of leadership in action. We can do well to learn the lessons that He taught through his life.

• A leadership activity (leadership experience) – Each chapter will also include a unique leadership activity designed to help you discover more about your leadership style. These are introspective activities that lead you through a series of questions to help you learn about yourself. What you discover may only confirm what you already know or it might be a fresh insight into how you lead. Either way, these activities will provide helpful feedback on your leadership abilities.

• Application questions – Finally, the chapter will end with several thought-provoking application questions. Be sure to spend some time with these questions. This section will give you the chance to respond to what you have learned and create action steps for making positive change. Knowledge only changes you when you apply it to your life.

How to use this book

This book was designed as a resource for you. We want to teach you leadership principles and help you learn more about your own leadership style. One way to use this book would be to read the narrative sections and complete the accompanying activities in each chapter. The opening sections will teach the leadership topic at hand. The activities will reinforce the topic and help you apply that principle to your leadership situation. Be sure to answer all the questions and complete all the activities. The power of this book lies in your ability to let it infiltrate all aspects of your leadership.

Another great use for this book is to provide direction for a mentoring relationship. If you don't have a mentor who can help you grow as a leader, we strongly urge you to find one. Any leader will tell you that having a mentor is indispensable to the process of developing your leadership abilities. Often, finding a mentor is as simple as asking a leader whom you respect to mentor you. Most leaders, when pursued, will respond favorably. Often, we fall victim to the trap of waiting for a mentor to approach us. Most likely, that will not happen. Pursue a mentoring relationship with a leader who is wiser than you. Then share with them what you are learning through this book. Their perspective will be invaluable to you. They will also be able to keep you accountable to the changes you commit to through the activities in this book. A mentor can also provide wise counsel when you face leadership challenges that seem overwhelming. Use this book as an excuse to find a mentor.

Finally, consider using this book as the basis of a challenging peer relationship with other youth workers or adult volunteers. Together, you can discuss the leadership topics and talk about how they apply to your ministry environment. You will learn much about each other as you discover your leadership styles together. Their perspective will help you identify issues in your leadership that you might not notice on your own. In short, learning together can be much more powerful than learning alone.

Remember that the goal is a balanced, effective leadership style. Becoming a better, more competent leader doesn't happen overnight. It requires focus and hard work. The outcome, however, will be more than worth it. Our hope is that the resources in this book start you on the road to becoming a more effective leader for God's Kingdom.

CHAPTER ONE

BALANCING THE TWO SIDES OF LEADERSHIP - DOING AND BEING

Chapter 1

Truman arrived at the church office on Tuesday morning, with his head already pounding. The morning cup of coffee hadn't even taken the edge off of his headache. I've got to get off of caffeine, he thought as he threw his empty cup in the trash. The real problem wasn't his headache. That was only a symptom. The problem was the youth ministry. Things just weren't working out the way he thought they would.

Truman had taken the job at First Community Church three years ago. It was his second job after graduation and he was sure that it would be a great fit. He had been at his first church for 4 years before moving to First Community. This church was in a great area and he and his new wife loved the senior pastor. The youth group that he took over was small but the students were committed. When he first met this group he was reminded of why he was attracted to youth ministry in the first place. He had enjoyed a great experience in his own youth group growing up. His youth pastor, Pastor Bob, was only part-time, but he had done a great job connecting with all the students and pouring into Truman specifically. Those were great times, he thought. Too bad Pastor Bob isn't here to give me some sage advice now.

Truman slumped into his chair, spun toward his computer, and, out of habit, logged onto his e-mail account. His body was going through the actions but his mind was elsewhere. He was still thinking about the weekend. "What a debacle." He said out loud to himself.

The weekend started with great promise. It was the big annual winter retreat. He had spent months working on the logistics for this event. Thirty-five students had signed up and all but two of them had paid ahead of time. That was a first! He had booked the camp and lined up the speaker. He had the adult volunteers in place and had fun activities to do all weekend. All in all, he felt he was ready.

When Friday night came, the problems started right away. First, a volunteer was an hour late because he had misunderstood the departure time. That caused the whole group to wait and they ended up an hour behind schedule. Then, the first night of the retreat, the senior guys decided to play pranks on the freshman guys. Things got out of control and one kid ended up duct taped to his bed for the better part of two hours. He was crushed and his parents were very upset. The next night two girls left their room and snuck into the guys' bunkhouse. Nothing happened but it certainly highlighted for Truman the lack of maturity that seemed to plague his ministry. In spite of all of these setbacks, Truman would have considered the trip a success if he had seen students making decisions leading to spiritual growth on the trip. While the speaker was excellent, it seemed like his kids were deaf to the message. Truman left the weekend incredibly discouraged.

It wasn't always this way, he thought. He had experienced more effective times during his early ministry years. Now, however, he seemed to have lost his way as a youth worker, and many of his problems seemed to be chronic. He had started to expect problems no matter what he planned or did. At his first church he had experienced these problems too, but he had assumed it was due to the negative environment he had endured there. Now the issues were resurfacing. He was the only common denominator. Maybe I need to rethink the root of my problems, he thought.

He was jolted back to reality as he looked at his computer screen. Besides the usual junk mail there were several e-mails from parents of students. He had a bad feeling about those messages. There was one from Josh's parents—the parents whose poor boy who had spent most of the night taped to his bed at the retreat. Truman had tried to find them at church on Sunday but they weren't there. I should have called them.

As he was contemplating what to do about that situation, he noticed an e-mail from Jerry. Jerry was the youth minister at the big Lutheran church down the street. He and Jerry knew each other from the monthly youth pastor network. Jerry had been in ministry for a long time, over 15 years. The first time they met, Truman thought that Jerry reminded him very much of his old youth pastor, Pastor Bob. When they saw each other, Truman and Jerry talked about sports and ministry. They had struck up a casual friendship. Now, in the midst of this crisis, Truman knew he needed Jerry's help.

Scanning the e-mail, Truman was surprised to read that Jerry wanted to get together with him and talk about doing an outreach together with his youth ministry. This is definitely a God thing, Truman thought as he responded to the e-mail. Jerry had suggested meeting at the coffee shop on Thursday morning. Thursday couldn't come fast enough for Truman. When Truman walked into the coffee shop that Thursday morning, his mind was heavy. The meeting with Josh's parents didn't go very well. Even though he had apologized, he recognized that he couldn't repair the hurt. They were considering moving to another church. Truman was preoccupied as he sat down in the booth across from Jerry.

"Great to see you," said Jerry. "Man, it's been a while. How's your ministry going?"

"It's been pretty rough lately. I might be looking for a new job soon." Truman responded.

"Wow, not exactly the response I was expecting. Is it something you want to talk about?" asked Jerry.

"Actually, that's exactly what I had in mind. I hope you don't mind if we put off planning the outreach event for a little while though," said Truman.

"Not at all," said Jerry. "We can work on that another time. Now, what's going on with you?"

"I don't even know where to begin," sighed Truman. "The big retreat that I had been planning for the last six months was a disaster. Parents are mad at me, my volunteers keep letting me down, and worst of all, I don't see God moving in the lives of my students anymore. I'm doing everything I can think of, and I can't figure out where I'm going wrong."

"Tell me more," said Jerry. Jerry listened intently as Truman explained his problems—starting with his first church and carrying over into his current position at First Community. Jerry listened and asked the occasional probing question as Truman described his challenges and victories in youth ministry. Even Truman was surprised at the number of challenges and the lack of victories from his ministry efforts.

"Sounds like kind of a bleak outlook." Jerry quipped after Truman had told his exhausting story.

"Yeah. I bet you've never had this many things go wrong in your youth ministry," said Truman.

"In fact, Truman, I was once in a much worse place than you. I felt like all I had done in ministry was coming unraveled. I looked at the situation long and hard and couldn't figure out what to do. It was then that a wise businessman in my church shared with me some advice that I think you need to learn." Jerry explained.

Truman almost exploded, "Don't leave me hanging! What's the secret?"

"Easy there, Truman. You might not like the answer because you probably already know it to be true. The secret he shared with me can be summed up in one phrase: 'Leadership changes everything.'"

"Sure," responded Truman, "I get that. But I have been leading and the real problem is that no one has been following me."

Jerry chuckled, "As a wise man once said, 'If you think you're leading and no one is following, then you are just taking a walk.' Your problem is not that you don't understand that leadership is important, it's that you don't value leadership enough."

"What do you mean?" asked Truman.

"I've been in ministry for over 15 years now and the lesson that I learn over and over is how important leadership really is. Think about your situation right now. Are you experiencing the same problems at First Community that you faced at your old church?" asked Jerry.

"Well, yeah, I guess so. I had already sort of noticed that." Truman quietly responded.

"You see," said Jerry, "when the problems keep following you, you can be pretty sure the source of those problems is you, not others. You need to focus on becoming a better leader. That is the most important thing you can do for your ministry."

"Gee, leadership seems like such an easy topic." said Truman with a sarcastic edge to his voice. "I wouldn't even know how to begin."

"I'll tell you what, Truman. I would be willing to teach you the same principles that my mentor taught me. These principles have helped my leadership grow in amazing ways. This week, let's start at the beginning. Leadership has two sides: doing and being." Jerry said.

"Sounds simple but what does that mean, exactly?" asked Truman.

"Well, the *doing* side of leadership is represented by what a leader does. These are the actions of leadership. They are things like casting vision, navigating obstacles, delegating responsibilities. Does that make sense?" asked Jerry.

"Sure, I get it. Those are all things a leader does. What does *being* mean in leadership?" asked a now-focused Truman.

"When we talk about *being* as it relates to leadership, we are talking about the characteristics of a leader. *Being* describes who a leader is on the inside. These are things like being teachable, having integrity, and valuing others more than yourself. So when you combine these two elements, you have the two sides of leadership: doing and being." Jerry explained.

"I've never thought about it that way. I really like the simplicity of it. But, let me ask you, Jerry, how does that apply to being a leader as a youth worker?" Truman asked.

"That's a great question and that's what I want you to work on. For the next week I want you to think about how much time you spend in each column. Pay attention to all the ways that you lead this week in your job and put them into a category, either doing or being. This will give you an idea of what you do well and what you need to work on." Jerry said.

"OK, I'll do it but I can already see how things will play out. I know that I spend way too much time on the doing and not enough time on the being. Keeping track will be revealing," explained Truman.

"Well, you aren't the only one with that problem," said Jerry, "Most leaders I know, including me, have a hard time with the being side of leadership. For more insight, take a look at the story of Jesus with Mary and Martha in Luke chapter 10. I bet our discussion here will give you some new eyes for that passage. Think through who focused on doing and who focused on being. Also, notice Jesus' response to both. Pretty fascinating stuff."

"Man, my brain is already full. You've given me a lot to think about. I really appreciate your help," Truman said.

"No problem. Let's get together next week to see how things are going. Before you leave I would love to pray for you," said Jerry.

After they prayed, Truman walked out to his car. For the first time in months he was excited. His conversation with Jerry had opened up his eyes to a whole new way of looking at his job. He hadn't realized how important it was for him to grow as a leader. In fact, according to Jerry, it was his most important job. As he drove to his office, he prayed that God would show him how to not only "do" leadership but how to "be" the best leader possible.

Leadership Principle:
Balancing the Two Sides of Leadership – Doing and Being

The importance of being an effective leader in youth ministry is hard to deny. You already believe that or you wouldn't be reading this book. The real question for you, just as it was for Truman, is how much do you really believe in the power of your leadership potential. You see, most youth workers agree that being a good leader is important. However, few are willing to do the hard work necessary to become a better leader. The truth is that the investment that you make in your own leadership potential might be the most important and effective investment that you can make for the students in your ministry.

As we look for a launching pad into effective leadership development, consider the two sides of leadership: doing and being. These are two aspects of leadership that we must hold in balance. We need to be leaders of action, represented by the doing side of leadership. Teams are motivated by accomplishing tasks and creating wins. Any effective leader needs to be one who is able to get things done.

At the same time successful leaders are those who understand the being side of leadership too. Leaders must cultivate their own personal character to have a true impact. Transformational leaders, those who invite their followers to create lasting change, are leaders who recognize that if they aren't growing, their followers won't grow either. The being side of leadership demands an investment in character. Most often leaders don't fail because of lack of skill; they fail because of lack of character.

Take a few minutes right now and read the story of Mary and Martha in Luke 10:38-41, then answer the following questions:

Martha represents the doing side of leadership. What are some the positive things she did in this passage? What did she miss?

_____

_____

_____

Mary represents the being side of leadership. How did she respond to Christ's presence?

_____

_____

_____

What was Jesus' response to these two women? What do you think He values more, doing or being? Why?

_____

_____

_____

Is it easier for you to focus on doing like Martha or being like Mary? Why?

_____

_____

_____

LeaderTreks

Doing vs. Being Assessment

The next exercise is designed to help you create a balance between doing and being in your leadership style. If you are like most leaders you can easily find yourself overwhelmed with the leadership tasks that you are required to do and spend very little time developing yourself as a leader. By examining the following areas of both the doing and the being side of leadership, you will be able to have a much clearer picture of how you spend your time and what you need to do to grow as a leader. Start by reading through each of the following lists and rating your performance in each area. Be honest, this is between you and God.

Rate yourself in every area below by writing a number between 1-10 to the left of each area. 1 = Needs a lot of work, 5 = Could use improvement and 10 = Needs no work.

Doing In Leadership

___Planning
___Organizing
___Evaluating
___Casting Vision
___Generating momentum
___Navigating obstacles
___Communicating
___Solving problems
___Managing others
___Developing teamwork
___Resolving conflict
___Focusing effort
___Risk taking
___Championing the cause
___Delegating
___Mentoring others
___Developing direction
___Encouraging
___Energizing the team
___Overcoming barriers

Being a leader

___Humble
___Committed
___Has Integrity
___Faithful
___Teachable
___Obedient
___Courageous
___Wise
___Compassionate
___Perseverant
___Loving
___Visionary
___Bold
___Discerning
___Values People
___Focused
___Motivating
___Consistent
___Thoughtful
___Meek

Now that you have evaluated both your doing and being side of leadership, do you notice any recurring themes? List those here.

_____
_____
_____

Next, circle the three areas of doing and the three areas of being that you most want to work on. They don't necessarily have to be your lowest scores. Instead, focus on the areas that will help you most in leadership in the near future.

ACTION PLAN
Doing leadership better

Create an action plan that will allow you to grow in the doing side of leadership.

List the three areas of doing that you want to grow in here.

_____

_____

_____

What is one thing you can do in each area to grow as a leader this week?

_____

_____

_____

How will you know if you are successful? How will you measure your growth?

_____

_____

ACCOUNTABILITY PLAN
Being a better leader

Work out an accountability plan that you can share with a trusted friend or mentor. This will allow you to work on the internal issues of leadership.

List the three areas of being that you want to grow in here.

_____

_____

_____

How can you develop these areas of your life?

_____

_____

_____

What situations will allow you to be stretched as a leader in these ways?

_____

_____

Who can keep you accountable to these changes?

_____

_____

Application

At the end of each chapter of this book we will take some time to apply the lessons to our lives. As you probably already recognize, only truth applied will change you. Our students often prove to us that just knowing a truth only takes you so far. It's when you choose to live that truth out that your life begins to change. Consider the following questions to help you apply this chapter to your life. *(Note: some of your answers may come from the previous Action Plan and Accoutability Plan)*

What has been the most important truth you have learned or that has been reinforced for you in this chapter?

_____

_____

_____

_____

What will you do this week to develop your character, the being side of your leadership?

_____

_____

_____

_____

What will you do this week to develop your skills as a leader, the doing side of leadership?

_____

_____

_____

_____

CHAPTER TWO

LIVING WITH INTEGRITY - THAT RUNS DEEPER THAN THE OBVIOUS

Chapter 2

The following week, Truman was preoccupied with thoughts resulting from his conversation with Jerry. Right after his last meeting with Jerry, he had gone back to his office and compared the amount of time he spent *doing* leadership as opposed to the amount of time he spent *being* a good leader. The results confirmed what he already knew. He was spending all of his time *doing* and very little time *being*. Even though he saw it coming, the cold hard truth was pretty depressing. He had been neglecting a very important leadership mandate, to develop his own inner life. Man, I've got some work to do, Truman thought to himself.

The week was hectic as usual. Truman had long since learned that ministry would demand his time more than anything else. However, as he went about his usual duties of planning for events, meeting with students, talking with volunteers, and studying for his talks, he noticed that his perspective started to shift. He was no longer going through the motions as he had just a week ago. Each leadership task that lay before him was now providing him an opportunity to focus not just on the *doing* side of leadership, but also on the *being*. It was as if he could feel himself awakening to ministry opportunities that were there all along. Best of all, he felt as if he was slowly beginning to develop his own leadership abilities again.

His wife, Lily, noticed the difference as well. Over breakfast a couple of days ago, she had said, "You seem much more energetic than usual. I haven't seen you this positive about the ministry in years. What's making the difference?"

Truman described his meeting with Jerry and all that he had learned during that hour in the coffee shop. "It's like someone has thrown a life line to a drowning man. I feel like there is hope for our ministry for the first time in a long time. Even more importantly, I think that Jerry has a lot to teach me about being a leader."

"I'm so glad you guys are connecting," said Lily. "I can't wait to see what else he has to teach you."

"I'll second that," said Truman. After talking it over with Lily, Truman realized that his interactions with Jerry had made a deeper impression on him than he first realized. He instinctively knew that this relationship was one that would mark him for a long time.

Truman pulled up to the coffee shop about fifteen minutes early. He wanted to spend some time reviewing the story from Luke 10 that Jerry had referenced last week. As he walked up to the counter to order his coffee, he was surprised to see Jerry already settled into a corner booth. After he waved to Jerry, he ordered and paid for his drink. He grabbed the cup, thanked the server, and walked over to the booth.

"Hey, I thought I was going to beat you here. Do you have a room in the back, or something?" Truman quipped.

"No," Jerry chuckled, "but I have been here for about an hour. I find this is a good place for me to think and pray. That can be hard to do at the office and almost impossible at home. A leader must be growing and this is the best place for me to do that."

Truman nodded in acknowledgement. He noticed the open Bible and the journal that Jerry was just putting to the side. "What are you working on right now?" asked Truman.

"Well, I'm always looking for new insights into leadership from God's Word. Nehemiah is one of my favorite books of scripture. I read through it again this morning and was journaling about how it applies to the leadership challenges that I am facing right now. Do you keep a journal?" asked Jerry

"Sometimes, but I'm not very good about being consistent with it."

"I understand that," replied Jerry. "It definitely is a discipline that must be cultivated. I would encourage you to start a leadership journal to record your thoughts as we go through this process. It will help give you clarity and it will also record the steps of growth you take so you can see the progress."

"OK, OK. I'm convicted. I will start one this week. Hey, I'm dying to find out the next *leadership secret* you have for me." Truman responded.

"Before we jump into that, tell me, what has stuck with you from our conversation last week?" Jerry asked.

"I was just talking about this same thing with my wife," Truman said "You know, I went back to my office after our meeting and I made out the list of how I have been spending my time, either in *doing* leadership or *being* a leader. I also paid much closer attention to leadership tasks and opportunities this week at work. My fears were confirmed. I spend almost all my time on leadership tasks and very little time, well maybe no time, on developing myself as a leader."

"So you're focused on the *doing* and not on the *being*" Jerry replied. "Well, you are not alone there. Most leaders I know struggle to find the balance. When we first start off in a leadership role we can only see the tasks that need to be done. We often don't realize the importance of developing ourselves. But, like I said last week, the investment you make in yourself is the most important investment you can make for your ministry."

"No need to convince me any further. I'm ready to figure out what to do about it," said Truman.

"OK then, let's look at the next step for you. This next leadership principle, like most important leadership truths, starts from within you. The truth that my mentor taught me is that leaders must have integrity. Integrity is the foundation for healthy, effective leadership."

"Well, yeah, that makes sense. Doesn't every leader already know that?" Truman asked.

"Oh, I think most people understand this principle but I don't know that everyone values it."

"What do you mean?" Truman asked. "We all know pastors who have fallen into moral failure or treasurers who have stolen money. These leaders didn't have integrity and it sunk them."

"I'm not just talking about the obvious areas that affect integrity, Truman," admonished Jerry. "I'm talking about having a value for integrity that impels you to make the tough calls no matter what the outcome. I define integrity as *doing the right things.*' Many leaders claim to have integrity but are afraid to stand on their own when they need to. Leadership is often about doing the difficult and unpopular things."

"OK, I'm starting to see the difference but I might need an example to clarify things."

"Alright, you mentioned that your winter retreat this year was a dud. What was the first thing to go wrong?"

"There were so many, it's kinda hard to remember," joked Truman. "Well, I guess the first thing that went wrong was when one of my volunteers showed up an hour late."

"That's a good example. Whose fault was it?" Jerry asked.

"It was clearly his," said Truman with a trace of anger in his voice. "All the kids knew when to be there and were on time. Why can't this grown adult show up on time? And it wasn't the first time he has been late. It's a pattern with him. The students had to wait an hour and the whole weekend schedule was thrown off."

"And how did you handle the situation? Did you talk to your volunteer about it?"

"Well…not directly," Truman mumbled. "I guess I sort of avoided the whole thing just to get the weekend started."

"Let me ask, did you sulk about it? Maybe give that volunteer the cold shoulder?" The look on Truman's face told the whole story for Jerry. "I guessed as much. You are not alone there either, Truman. Many leaders resort to what I call *passive aggressive leadership* when things aren't going their way. This is a great example of what I mean by having integrity in your leadership. Were you proud of the way you handled this leadership challenge?"

"Of course not," Truman responded. "I felt terrible but it was already too late."

"It's never too late. You always have a chance to redeem yourself. In fact, integrity in leadership shows through strongest when you can admit your mistake and ask a follower to forgive you. Think about how strong your relationship might be with your volunteer if you had apologized for your attitude. He would have learned to trust you and you could have addressed the behavior that caused the problem in the first place."

"Yeah, I know you're right. I just never realized that my integrity was at stake."

"I think you are starting to see it now," said Jerry, smiling. "Here's the other thing about integrity: it's best displayed through a Godly character. You remember the fruit of the spirit, right? Love, joy, peace, patience, kindness, goodness, faithfulness, gentleness, and self-control. Well, you can show your integrity as a leader by living out those characteristics."

"That makes sense. When I hear that list I know that I still have a lot to work on. Can you think of any other examples from scripture that might help me develop the integrity of a leader?" asked Truman.

"One of my favorite passages on integrity," replied Jerry "is one you might not think of. It's the story of Jesus in the garden of Gethsemane. Jesus is a great example of integrity and character in action. Even in the most trying time of his life, he still chose to do the right thing. The scripture in Matthew 26 shows the depth of his commitment as he contemplated the death that was before him."

"That's definitely humbling," Truman said. "I'm going to look at that story this week. Any other homework?"

"Definitely. Start your leadership journal this week. Spend some time examining your character as a leader. Don't just focus on the weaknesses but also list the strengths. Next week we can talk about some of the things you learned."

After they prayed together, Truman thanked Jerry for his time and headed for the door. He was so focused that he didn't even think to grab a cup of coffee for the road. No big deal, he thought. As he got into his car, he looked back at the coffee shop. Through the window, he saw Jerry deep in thought with the journal once again opened before him. Truman could hardly wait until next week.

Leadership Principle:
Living With Integrity that Runs Deeper than the Obvious

Integrity is the bedrock of strong, effective, and Godly leadership. You probably already agree with this statement but maybe you are like Truman and think that integrity is just related to moral issues. It's true that the integrity of a leader is revealed during a moral crisis; however, being a leader of integrity means so much more than that.

As a leader, your integrity is tested all the time. You are often forced to choose between doing the easy thing and doing the right thing. How you handle these challenging situations will make or break you as a leader. Being a leader of integrity requires a focused effort to grow your character in all situations.

Jesus also faced many challenges to the integrity of His leadership. From the attacks of the Pharisees to the questions of His own disciples, Jesus stayed true to his mission and did the right thing every time. Open your Bible to Matthew 26:36-46 and review the story of Jesus in the garden of Gethsemane. Think through the following questions.

What were the emotions that Jesus was feeling at this time in His life? Have you ever had similar feelings?

_____

_____

_____

_____

What does this passage teach us about the character of Jesus' leadership?

_____

_____

_____

_____

What do you think sustained Jesus during this time?

_____

_____

_____

_____

What lessons can you apply to your own leadership situation from this passage?

_____

_____

_____

_____

Leadership Experience:
The LeaderTreks Building Character Profile

The strength of a leader's integrity is often evidenced by the outgrowth of Godly characteristics. The fruit of the Spirit that Paul outlined in Galatians 5:22 give us a great list of Godly characteristics that all leaders should strive to emulate. The LeaderTreks Building Character Profile will help you examine your own leadership character in light of the fruit of the Spirit. This assessment will reveal areas of your life that need to be addressed. It will also assess three areas we call "readiness to change" indicators. These indicators—attitude, awareness, and accountability—will govern any change to your character that you are trying to make. You must be aware of the changes that are needed, have an attitude that is positive toward change, and the accountability from other believers to make it happen. Work through this assessment and share the results with a friend or mentor.

Building Character Profile

As with skills, character develops as a result of consistent practice supported by appropriate feedback. Character-building is a lifelong pursuit. No one ever arrives at that point where they have no aspects of character needing further improvement. In fact, a key to developing Christian character is having the attitude that you can always become better. You do that through a combination of obedience to God's commands and prayerful reliance on the work of the Holy Spirit in you.

This profile is designed to help you become more aware of where you currently are on key aspects of Christian character. As with any such survey, your results will only be as accurate as the answers you give. Be sure to answer based on who you really are, not who you would like to be or who others think you ought to be.

Read the following statements carefully. Enter your ratings on the response sheet based on how well the statement describes you, using the following scale:

5	Always true of me
4	Almost always true
3	Often true of me
2	Occasionally true
1	Seldom or never true

		Always true of me	Almost always true	Often true of me	Occasionally true	Seldom or never true
1.	I want to demonstrate my love for God by continually growing in character, seeking to be more like Jesus.	5	4	3	2	1
2.	I assess my behavior against my expectations regarding character, and compare myself with people I see as positive role models.	5	4	3	2	1
3.	I think others see me as someone who is open to honest feedback about matters of character, and who sincerely tries to act on their insights and suggestions.	5	4	3	2	1
4.	I want to show love to others by doing what is best for them, without any need for appreciation, recognition, or repayment in return.	5	4	3	2	1
5.	No matter what circumstances I find myself in, I am able to overcome fear and doubt and find some cause for joy in my situation.	5	4	3	2	1
6.	I think others see me as a peacemaker, helping others to heal broken relationships or to restore a sense of order and harmony to their lives.	5	4	3	2	1
7.	I strive to manage my anger or frustration in healthy ways, honestly sharing my feelings while seeking a constructive resolution to the situation that caused them.	5	4	3	2	1
8.	I tune in to the basic needs of people, even those others overlook or avoid, and find ways to come alongside them and provide practical support.	5	4	3	2	1
9.	I think others see me as someone with a sincere desire to follow God's will, ready to do what is necessary to achieve the greatest good in any given situation.	5	4	3	2	1

		Always true of me	Almost always true	Often true of me	Occasionally true	Seldom or never true
10.	It is important to me to be a person that others can trust, relying on me to keep my promises, fulfill my commitments, and remain loyal in my relationships.	5	4	3	2	1
11.	I approach difficult situations and people in a gentle way that reduces tension and conflict, and creates a climate conducive to resolving problems.	5	4	3	2	1
12.	I think others see me as someone who is sincerely and consistently striving to live out my most important beliefs and principles in my daily actions.	5	4	3	2	1
13.	I actively seek to grow in character through obedience to God's word and prayerful reliance on the Holy Spirit.	5	4	3	2	1
14.	I think others see me as someone with clear, appropriate expectations of myself regarding character, and an accurate, honest self-assessment of my behavior.	5	4	3	2	1
15.	I see the importance of being open to feedback from others about matters of character, and want people to feel that they can be honest with me in this area.	5	4	3	2	1
16.	I demonstrate love to others, even those whom others avoid, by meeting their practical needs, without concern for my help being deserved or repaid.	5	4	3	2	1
17.	I think others see me as someone who has a consistent underlying sense of joy and satisfaction rooted in my close personal relationship with Jesus Christ.	5	4	3	2	1

		Always true of me	Almost always true	Often true of me	Occasionally true	Seldom or never true
18.	It is important to me to seek peace and harmony in my relationships with God and others, and between others, pursuing reconciliation where necessary.	5	4	3	2	1
19.	When I feel myself getting angry or frustrated, I identify the cause of my feelings and seek to express them in healthy ways that support problem-solving.	5	4	3	2	1
20.	I think others see me as someone who has a real heart for others, and who is quick to respond in practical ways to meet their basic personal needs.	5	4	3	2	1
21.	I want to do the right thing regardless of circumstances, striving to understand God's will and consistently acting according to Christian principles.	5	4	3	2	1
22.	I realize that the trust of others must be earned, and I strive to demonstrate my trustworthiness by being consistently loyal and dependable.	5	4	3	2	1
23.	I think others see me as humble, yet quietly confident in my ability to handle difficult situations effectively with strength, calmness, and a gentle spirit.	5	4	3	2	1
24.	I want to live my life with a sense of direction and self-discipline, where my thoughts and actions consistently reflect my beliefs and principles.	5	4	3	2	1
25.	I think others see me as someone who is actively striving to grow as a Christian, genuinely seeking to be more like Jesus.	5	4	3	2	1

		Always true of me	Almost always true	Often true of me	Occasionally true	Seldom or never true
26.	I want to have a realistic assessment of my own character, understanding my strengths and those areas needing further development.	5	4	3	2	1
27.	I work to build open, trusting relationships with selected individuals with whom I can honestly discuss matters of character, and seek feedback and advice.	5	4	3	2	1
28.	I think others see me as someone who unselfishly cares for people, seeking the best for them without needing to receive anything in return.	5	4	3	2	1
29.	I hope others can see the deep sense of spiritual satisfaction I experience, even in difficult times, because of the joy I get from my relationship with Jesus Christ.	5	4	3	2	1
30.	I take practical steps to achieve and maintain peace, order, and harmony in my life, and to support others seeking to do the same.	5	4	3	2	1
31.	I think others see me as someone who is slow to anger, able to express my feelings constructively while focusing on solving the problems that caused them.	5	4	3	2	1
32.	It is important to me to "be there" for others, valuing them as people, seeking to understand their needs, and caring enough to help in practical ways.	5	4	3	2	1
33.	I avoid taking the easy way out of challenging situations, preferring to do the right thing as determined by an honest, careful assessment of God's will.	5	4	3	2	1

		Always true of me	Almost always true	Often true of me	Occasionally true	Seldom or never true
34.	I think others see me as someone who is dependable and reliable, having earned the trust of others by consistently following through on my commitments.	5	4	3	2	1
35.	I strive to find an appropriate balance of strength with humility, handling difficult situations and people gently, confidently, and effectively.	5	4	3	2	1
36.	I recognize the reality of the daily struggle between self-discipline and self-indulgence, and strive to live out my Christian values more and more fully.	5	4	3	2	1

Totals

1	13	25		1. ____
2	14	26		2. ____
3	15	27		3. ____
4	16	28		4. ____
5	17	29		5. ____
6	18	30		6. ____
7	19	31		7. ____
8	20	32		8. ____
9	21	33		9. ____
10	22	34		10. ____
11	23	35		11. ____
12	24	36		12. ____

Scoring Guide

Enter your scores from the response sheet by placing a dot over the appropriate number for each aspect of character. Then connect the dots with a line to reflect your scoring pattern Consider any score in single digits to be in the danger zone.

	Gift	Description				
1.	Attitude	Loving God and wanting to emulate His character in your thoughts and actions	1	5	10	15 ++
2.	Awareness	Accurately identifying your character strengths and areas needing further development	1	5	10	15 ++
3.	Accountability	Seeking feedback from others on matters of character and acting on it	1	5	10	15 ++
4.	Love	Loving others by unselfishly seeking what is best for them	1	5	10	15 ++
5.	Joy	Having a deep, lasting sense of spiritual satisfaction regardless of your circumstances	1	5	10	15 ++
6.	Peace	Being at peace with God, yourself, and others, even in the midst of turmoil	1	5	10	15 ++
7.	Patience	Managing your feelings of anger or frustration in a healthy, productive way	1	5	10	15 ++
8.	Kindness	Helping others in practical ways that demonstrate genuine concern for their well-being	1	5	10	15 ++

9.	**Goodness**	Doing the right thing, according to God's will, regardless of circumstances	1	5	10	15 ++
10.	**Faithfulness**	Keeping promises and being loyal in order to earn the trust of others	1	5	10	15 ++
11.	**Gentleness**	Projecting a spirit of humility and quiet confidence even in challenging situations	1	5	10	15 ++
12.	**Self-control**	Living your life with integrity and discipline, seeking increasing self-mastery	1	5	10	15 ++

Note: The scoring graph extends beyond the 15 possible points for each indicator to show that we never fully arrive and should always be striving to grow in character and become more and more like Christ.

This profile is based on the nine character qualities listed in the fruit of the Spirit. Additionally, three important factors have been included: attitude, awareness, and accountability. Together, these twelve indicators provide a way for you to identify and address character development.

But the fruit of the Spirit is love, joy, peace, patience, kindness, goodness, faithfulness, gentleness and self-control.
Galatians 5:22-23 (NIV)

The following pages take a deeper look at these twelve aspects of character. Take a look at each one and then begin making some application steps at the end of this chapter.

Attitude

Basic Definition
Loving God and wanting to emulate His character in your thoughts and actions.

Importance
The essential first step in developing godly character is to decide that it is important to you. This means looking up to God, taking your relationship with Him seriously, and wanting to do His will. The Bible makes it clear that this begins with loving God, who first loved you. In gratitude, you are to commit yourself to becoming more like Jesus, your ultimate role model.

When you fail to make this commitment, the result is that your growth as a believer is stunted and your witness is compromised. This is because you are unsure of what is important to you, living without clear standards to guide your behavior, and disconnected from the source of the power you need to live an authentic Christian life.

This Dimension in Scripture
You were taught, with regard to your former way of life, to put off your old self, which is being corrupted by its deceitful desires; to be made new in the attitude of your minds; and to put on the new self, created to be like God in true righteousness and holiness.
Ephesians 4:22-25 (NIV)

Tips for Growth
The fruit of the Spirit is singular--it isn't a collection of character traits from which you can pick and choose the ones that are most comfortable or that you think might be most noticeable to others. A commitment to character-building must include all aspects. This inventory identifies three success factors (attitude, awareness, accountability), along with the nine aspects spiritual fruit listed in Galatians 5:23-23. Focus on the whole. Acknowledge both your strengths and those areas you need to work on.

It is also important that you understand character-building is a lifelong responsibility. Each stage of life brings new challenges and new opportunities to learn and grow. Finally, you need to know that this process requires both your own active participation in obedience to God's will and His support through prayerful reliance on the power of His Spirit. Without both, sustained growth cannot happen.

Awareness

Basic Definition

Accurately identifying your character strengths and areas needing further development.

Importance

In any area where you want to grow, you first need to understand your starting point. This means looking in to understand who you are at your best and your worst. Then you can determine what action to take and you will also be better able to pray for wisdom, direction, and the strength to act.

When awareness is low, the result is a very human tendency toward self-deception and self-justification. This is usually accompanied by a focus on others' words or actions, particularly their perceived shortcomings, which are then used to explain why certain problems are occurring or to justify your own behavior.

This Dimension in Scripture

If anyone thinks he is something when he is nothing, he deceives himself. Each one should test his own actions. Then he can take pride in himself, without comparing himself to somebody else, for each one should carry his own load.
Galatians 6:3-6 (NIV)

Tips for Growth

Awareness doesn't come automatically. As with every aspect of character building, you must decide to do something about it. On the obedience side, that means learning about the twelve aspects of character building addressed in this inventory. You need to understand each aspect at a deep personal level, and appreciate its importance. Think about situations in your life where each aspect is particularly important, and honestly assess your current performance. Identify people you know who are positive role models for each aspect and observe what they are doing more effectively than you.

It is also vitally important to recognize that there is a real spiritual battle going on—an ongoing battle against a real enemy. Ask God to protect you in this battle, and put on the spiritual armor described in the Bible (Ephesians 6:10-18). Invite God to reveal to you the truth about you, both positive and negative, and to provide good role models from whom you can learn.

Accountability

Basic Definition
Seeking feedback from others on matters of character and acting on it.

Importance
Often others are able to see--or challenge us to see--aspects of our behavior that we cannot. Real accountability is looking to others who know and care about you and inviting them to help you with matters of the heart. This is especially true with situations you find difficult to discuss or habits you haven't been able to break. Open sharing with a trusted friend or mentor can be a key part of gaining the insight you need into your behavior and why things aren't working as they should. It can also provide the support you need to take courageous action or commit to significant change.

When accountability is missing, it is easy to avoid facing important areas of your thinking or behavior that might really be holding you back in your growth as a believer or causing unnecessary problems for yourself and others. At its worst, it can lead to elaborate defensive patterns that can prevent you from confronting important issues you need to address.

This Dimension in Scripture
Test me, O LORD, and try me, examine my heart and my mind; for your love is ever before me, and I walk continually in your truth.
Psalm 26:2-3 (NIV)

Tips for Growth
Character development is a team sport—it isn't something that most of us can do on our own. That's why we all need accountability. You need to find the right person or group—people you trust with your innermost thoughts and who you believe want only the best for you—so you will feel free to share openly. If you don't already have people like that in your life, begin to look for them now. As you identify people with whom you might be able to form an accountability relationship, you need to be ready to be open and honest with them and to encourage them to give you feedback. Tell them about the areas in which you are trying to grow and invite them to help you by providing feedback, suggestions, and prayer support. Above all, honor the feedback you receive by acting on it.

At the same time, ask God to develop in you a spirit of humility and openness and to bring others into your life as potential accountability partners.

Love

Basic Definition
Loving others by unselfishly seeking what is best for them.

Importance
The only reason that any believer should need for making love a priority is that Jesus commands you to do so. Love is at the heart of the greatest commandment--loving God, yourself, your neighbors, and even your enemies. It is the defining characteristic of a Christian.

When love is missing, selfishness rules. Your concern is more for your own needs than those of others. You worry about whether you are being treated fairly, comparing what you are getting with what you believe you are giving. Even when you are trying to show love to others, it is still all about you.

This Dimension in Scripture
By this all men will know that you are my disciples, if you love one another.
John 13:35 (NIV)

Tips for Growth
The *agape* love that Jesus commands us to demonstrate requires that you put the needs of others above your own. This means that sometimes you'll be acting in ways that don't happen naturally. Remember, love is a choice. You must be very intentional about what you must do and why you are doing it. You also need to become involved with others closely enough to see their real needs so that you can respond appropriately. Finally, you must learn to love the unlovely—not to mention the ungrateful. This is the truest test of your willingness to follow Christ's command.

Ask God to give you a tender heart like His and to help you look beyond your own needs—and others' faults—to see the needs of others. At the same time, give thanks to God for having done exactly that in showing His love to you. By acknowledging what you have received, it will become easier to show the same love to others.

Joy

Basic Definition
Having a deep, lasting sense of spiritual satisfaction regardless of your circumstances.

Importance
Joy is all about perspective—seeing the glass half full versus half empty. It is what tells others that God has done something special in your life, making it possible to sustain a deep sense of wellbeing despite whatever difficulties you are facing. As such, joy validates faith. Happiness may be fleeting, but joy persists. It also sustains you through the dark times and helps you to hold onto hope and to continue to look for the Lord's goodness even in times of sorrow.

When joy is missing, the result is discouragement, dissatisfaction, and eventually a bitterness that prevents you from seeing God's hand at work in your own life and makes others doubt the value of your faith.

This Dimension in Scripture
Rejoice in the Lord always, I will say it again: Rejoice!
Philippians 4:4 (NIV)

Tips for Growth
A good starting point is to count your blessings daily. Take time to do so even when you don't really feel like it. In dark times, develop the habit of remembering the ways in which God has carried you through those times in the past and let your outlook be brightened by those faith memories. Finally, you should always be ready to express your joy to others and to explain its source.

Also, ask God to help you to transcend your circumstances, freeing you from fear, doubt, and guilt so you can hold on to the deep joy you feel being His beloved child. Give thanks for His faithful concern for you in both the good times and bad. Invite Him to make His presence clear to you when you are facing difficulties or sorrow.

Peace

Basic Definition
Being at peace with God, yourself, and others, even in the midst of turmoil.

Importance
Peace and reconciliation are at the center of God's plan. This includes peace *with* God by accepting His free gift of salvation through Jesus Christ. But it also includes having the peace of God, the inner sense of tranquility in the midst of conflict or confusion, and God's peace on earth, the peace that can only come when people are reconciled to one another. God wants us to be peacemakers—people who experience peace in our own lives in all of these ways and who help others to find it as well.

When peace is missing, discord and confusion increase creating uncertainty and anxiety. This, in turn, causes people to speak and act in ways which cause more discord and confusion, creating an endless cycle of deterioration.

This Dimension in Scripture
If it is possible, as far as it depends on you, live at peace with everyone.
Romans 12:18 (NIV)

Tips for Growth
One of the first requirements of being a peacemaker is to think about where you may be sowing seeds of discord or confusion as you fight for your own rights or defend your own views. Then, seek reconciliation with those your actions have affected and work with them to find win-win solutions to your shared problems. This can free you up to be a peacemaker who can help others to seek fair and just solutions to conflicts and other divisive problems.

At the same time, ask God to make you sensitive to your impact on others and to guide your actions so that you don't cause discord or confusion--even unknowingly. Where you see broken relationships, pray for reconciliation and ask God to show you how you can help bring this about.

Patience

Basic Definition
Managing your feelings of anger or frustration in a healthy, productive way.

Importance
If you have ever found yourself wishing you could take back a hasty word or action, you know that patience is a key element of maintaining a consistent witness as a follower of Christ. This is especially true when dealing with difficult people or situations. Patience is not a matter of suppressing or repressing legitimate anger and frustration, pretending that those feelings don't exist. Rather, it is about expressing those feelings in constructive ways. Patience is what gives you the time and space you need to seek workable solutions to important problems or conflicts.

When patience is missing, the result is pain—for yourself or others—which inevitably leads to more anger and frustration all around. Eventually, this causes everyone involved to focus on self-protection, creating both distance and resistance in your relationships, and undermining your ability to work together constructively.

This Dimension in Scripture
And we urge you, brothers, warn those who are idle, encourage the timid, help the weak, be patient with everyone.
1 Thessalonians 5:14 (NIV)

Tips for Growth
Begin by realizing that anger is not a sin, but our reaction to those feelings may be. When you sense these feelings building inside you, take time to identify their cause and to determine an appropriate response. Learn to express these feelings constructively. Look for the right time, place, and manner in which to communicate with the right people.

Also, ask God to help you to control your anger or frustration—to resist simply reacting—and to help you respond to difficult people or situations with understanding, restraint, and compassion.

Kindness

Basic Definition
Helping others in practical ways that demonstrates genuine concern for their well-being.

Importance
Burden-bearing is the gospel in action at its most fundamental level. You've heard the saying that your actions are the first gospel that others read. If that is true, then it could be said that kindness is what establishes your credibility as a follower of Christ in the eyes of others. Indeed, Jesus described various acts of kindness as the key indicators of whether someone was truly one of His followers (Matthew 25).

When kindness is missing, indifference reigns causing loneliness and alienation, particularly for those least able to speak up for themselves. Lack of kindness can lead to a "careless community"—a place where people couldn't care less. You have an obligation to push back against this kind of debilitating indifference.

This Dimension in Scripture
Be kind and compassionate to one another, forgiving each other, just as in Christ God forgave you.
Ephesians 4:32 (NIV)

Tips for Growth
The starting point for growing in kindness is to take the time to tune-in to others' basic personal needs. Try to understand their situation from their perspective, and then look for the often simple ways in which you can share their load. When people experience disappointment or failure, look for ways to provide a soft place for them to fall.

At the same time, ask God to help you look beyond your own needs, or others' shortcomings, to see their real needs. Pray for the compassion to care and the courage to act, especially where doing so seems particularly inconvenient or even risky.

Goodness

Basic Definition
Doing the right thing, according to God's will, regardless of circumstances.

Importance
Goodness is not about feeling good, living the good life, or having a good time. This aspect of the fruit of the Spirit involves seeking the greater good, being an advocate for truth, justice and mercy. It means doing the right thing, whether or not it is the easy or popular course of action. Goodness is holding fast to the principles that you say are important to you as a believer, whatever the consequences.

When goodness is missing, sin reigns. You are tempted to abuse your freedom, position or influence to do what is right in your own eyes, and to acquire what you want—even at the expense of others.

This Dimension in Scripture
Do not conform any longer to the pattern of this world, but be transformed by the renewing of your mind. Then you will be able to test and approve what God's will is—his good, pleasing and perfect will.
Romans 12:2 (NIV)

Tips for Growth
Goodness requires you to be able to discern God's will in the circumstances in which you find yourself, and that means being familiar with His expectations as revealed in the Bible. The more clearly you understand the core principles of leading a godly life, the easier it will be for you to know what must be done in a given situation. Become a student of God's word, and take time to think through specific applications of His principles in your life.

Ask God to help give you the wisdom to know what is required, and the courage to act on this insight, especially when your actions may be unpopular or unpleasant. Pray for a deep desire to seek the greater good. Pursue it without becoming begrudging or envious when doing the right thing for those you may feel are undeserving.

Faithfulness

Basic Definition
Keeping promises and being loyal in order to earn the trust of others.

Importance
Faithfulness is the ground on which faith rests. If you think about it, your faith in God has grown as you have experienced His faithfulness in your own life or seen it in His ongoing concern for others. Your faithfulness has the same effect on others that look to rely on you for love, support, direction, or any number of other practical needs. Trust is earned and continually validated by acting in ways that demonstrate your trustworthiness. In relationships, this means demonstrating your loyalty to the other person, especially in trying circumstances.

When faithfulness is missing, not only will others lose trust in you, but often will find it harder to trust others in the future. Recall your own experience of someone letting you down and you will realize the long-term effects that this can have. It can take a long time to be able to trust again. Your faithfulness, on the other hand, can sustain and build others' trust in you and in God.

This Dimension in Scripture
Now it is required that those who have been given a trust must prove faithful.
1 Corinthians 4:2 (NIV)

Tips for Growth
For starters, take care that you don't make promises you can't be sure you will keep. Think carefully before you make commitments, then work hard to demonstrate your reliability in following through. Seek increased responsibility as a way of challenging yourself to improve your reliability and follow-through capacity. Invite others to hold you accountable for keeping your commitments and seek their feedback on how you are doing.

At the same time, ask God to strengthen your resolve to follow through on your commitments, especially when no one is watching or where you feel pressured to compromise.

Gentleness

Basic Definition
Projecting a spirit of humility and quiet confidence even in challenging situations.

Importance
Gentleness is not weakness or passivity, but rather an aspect of character that is necessary to create an environment where the truth can be spoken and honored. Gentleness makes it possible for you and others to pursue noble ends instead of defending personal positions or rights. It has a calming effect that makes true dialogue and deeper understanding possible.

When gentleness is missing, relationships are characterized by intimidation with all parties concerned more for self-preservation or winning than for building consensus and seeking solutions that are good for everyone involved.

This Dimension in Scripture
Those who oppose him he must gently instruct, in the hope that God will grant them repentance leading to a knowledge of the truth.
2 Timothy 2:25 (NIV)

Tips for Growth
Your first goal should be to identify your unique challenges in this area. For some people it is a tendency to become aggressive in advocating their own viewpoints. For others it is a pattern of caving—in or going silent when challenged to express their opinions. Your goal is to learn to temper the strength of your convictions with a gentle spirit, to find the middle ground between aggressiveness and indifference. This will give you the capacity and earn you the right to tell the truth in love.

You should also ask God to help you focus on achieving the right ends rather than defending your own position when you find yourself in conflict with others. At those times, pray for quiet confidence in your ability to contribute to finding a constructive solution as well as a calming manner in how you go about it.

Self-control

Basic Definition
Living your life with integrity and discipline, seeking increasing self-mastery.

Importance
Without self-control, growth is impossible. Self-control leads to greater levels of mastery in whatever areas you choose to grow, as well as greater confidence in your ability to tackle those areas that are more difficult for you. You have probably noticed that it is relatively easy for you to keep working on developing your strengths. But the real test of self-control is in applying it to areas where your performance is poorest. These are the areas where you most need to discipline yourself to bring the flesh into submission to your spirit.

When self-control is missing, the result is self-indulgence and mediocrity. Self-indulgence is attractive because it focuses your attention on what feels comfortable to you. Mediocrity is attractive because it is so much easier. These temptations cause us to grow steadily weaker until even our former strengths are compromised.

This Dimension in Scripture
Rather, clothe yourselves with the Lord Jesus Christ, and do not think about how to gratify the desires of the sinful nature.
Romans 12:1 (NIV)

Tips for Growth
Identify the areas you want to work on. Don't take on too much, and don't start you're your toughest challenges. Instead, start with those areas where you feel most confident of success and ready to make a commitment to grow. Begin by setting clear, concrete goals for growth and making appropriate plans to achieve them. Make sure your plans include timelines and checkpoints. Tell others about your goals and plans, and seek their support in following through. Move forward with steady, disciplined action and monitor and celebrate your progress.

Ask God to give you wisdom as you select areas to work on and develop your plans. Pray also for the courage and strength you'll need to overcome procrastination, distraction, discouragement, and other barriers that could cause you to abandon your goals.

Application

Looking over your scores, you probably recognize some aspects of Christian character that you need to develop. If you are like most people, you probably want to tackle your lowest areas first. Don't! You could end up in that uncomfortable situation many of us know well from our annual experience with New Year's resolutions.

Here are some steps for deciding which areas to tackle first, and which to leave for later.

STEP ONE

Start by reviewing your scores on the first three dimensions: attitude, awareness and accountability. To succeed in strengthening any aspect of character, you need to be doing well on all three of these factors.

List any of these where your scores are in the danger zone (a score of 0-9 on the graph).

_____
_____
_____
_____

These are your logical starting points. Developing your character will be difficult if you don't love God, don't want to emulate the character of Jesus, can't identify areas needing development accurately, or don't want feedback from others. In the process of character development, Attitude is reaching up, Awareness is reaching in, and Accountability is reaching out for help.

STEP TWO

Make a plan for strengthening these areas before moving on to other areas. If you scored low on Attitude, consider what steps you could take to improve in the areas of obedience and reliance. If you scored low on Awareness, think of ways you could become more tuned-in to yourself on matters of character. If you scored low on Accountability, consider what you could do to establish an effective accountability relationship as an essential step toward character-building.

List some key steps in your plan below.

_____
_____
_____
_____

Next, you need to identify which of the nine aspects of the fruit of the Spirit you will focus on once you've taken the steps listed in Lesson One and moved all of the first three dimensions out of the danger zone. Again, the best starting point is often not your lowest scoring dimension.

As we discovered in Lesson One, a helpful concept for deciding what to focus on next is readiness for change. We are all more ready for change in some areas of our life than others. Readiness for change principles were discovered by studying how people have succeeded in overcoming unhealthy or annoying habits, achieving important goals, or successfully handling difficult challenges. In short, people are most successful when they understand their degree of readiness for change and act accordingly.

Here are the stages that describe levels of readiness for change:

- **Avoiding:** not really a priority, often a result of ignorance, indifference, or denial
- **Considering:** not motivated enough to change but no longer able to ignore or deny
- **Learning:** open to exploring what needs to change and why that might be important
- **Planning:** setting the stage for change by taking steps to prepare to take action
- **Acting:** taking appropriate steps to achieve change and monitoring your progress
- **Maintaining:** continuing to do the things you know are essential to sustaining change
- **Rebuilding:** honestly admitting when you relapse and restarting the process of change

Honestly review your scores on the nine aspects of the fruit of the Spirit and select two or three where you are at least at the Learning stage of readiness. We know that this is the minimal level for standing a good chance of being successful. Then, in the space below, list some specific steps you can take to begin to move forward.

What do you need to do in terms of Learning, Planning and Acting? (Or Maintaining and Rebuilding if you're focusing on an area where you already have been taking effective action.) Select no more than three aspects of character as you begin this process.

a) _____

b) _____

c) _____

Finally, meet with someone with whom you are in an accountability relationship, and invite that person to help you to review your choices, refine your plans, and begin to take action. Commit yourself to specific goals, a timeline, and feedback appointments.

CHAPTER THREE

EMBRACING HUMILTTY

Chapter 3

Truman sat on the hill overlooking the lake and admired the sunshine on the blue water. This was a great way to spend his day off. He loved coming here in the summer time and watching the activity on the lake below. The hike to this hilltop was a strenuous two and a half miles from the trailhead. Not too many other people were willing to make the effort today. That was just fine for Truman. He wanted to be alone anyway.

Glancing down at the journal in his lap he started thinking about his week. He was trying to be more observant of the leadership opportunities that were coming his way. He never realized how many he had until he started writing them down. This week had taught him some pretty tough lessons on what it means to do, as Jerry said, 'the right things'.

Take what happened on Sunday, when Brad, a parent, cornered him. "Hey, can I share a concern with you, Truman?"

This can't be good, Truman thought to himself. "Sure, what's up?"

"Well, my son, Jason, is telling me that youth group is boring. He doesn't want to come anymore. I think you should try to spice things up. Maybe more concerts and games. I bet if you got the parents together we could come up with some good ideas."

Truman was flabbergasted. Not only was Brad making his job harder by creating more activities for him to plan and run, he was actually suggesting that studying the Bible and growing as a Christian weren't interesting enough for his child. Truman was proud of the fact that his youth group didn't have a lot of "fluff" activities. With his limited time, Truman wanted to focus on what he thought really mattered.

"Listen, Brad," Truman started, "I'm surprised to hear that Jason has such a strong opinion about our youth ministry. He never seems to be paying attention as far as I can tell. Besides, I have chosen to focus on the things that matter and not spend time with stuff that is just a waste of time."

"Hey, my kid's opinion is important. It's not a waste of time. This is why kids don't want to be a part of your youth ministry. You won't even listen to them!" Brad exploded. "I'm going to take this up with the elder committee."

"That's not what I meant. But the truth is, as the leader I have to do what I think is right," Truman responded.

Brad gave him a sour look and strode away. I'm probably going to hear about that one Truman thought. The conversation nagged him the rest of the day. He wished he could do it over again. In that moment, Brad's comments had made him so angry. He felt hurt and betrayed when parents attacked his choices like this. But in his heart he knew he could have handled the situation better.

His thoughts shifted back to the present as he gazed on the lake below him. Tomorrow he was going to meet with Jerry again. He was learning so much from this ministry veteran. Truman couldn't wait to talk over this new problem with him. He was sure that Jerry could shed some light on how to handle disgruntled parents. Jerry called earlier in the week to set up their appointment. He told Truman to set aside a whole afternoon this week. I wonder what he's got up his sleeve, Truman thought to himself.

The two youth workers met in the parking lot of Jerry's church. Truman was just getting out of his car when Jerry strode up to him. "Let's take a ride," suggested Jerry.

As they got in Jerry's car and drove out of the parking lot, Truman asked, "Where are we going?"

"You'll see," said Jerry. "I don't want to spoil the surprise but I promise it will be worth your time."

They made small talk as they drove into the city, learning more about each other and how they each got into ministry. As they drove, Truman watched the neighborhoods they were passing. He had heard about some of these areas on the evening news but he had never been here himself. They were driving through a pretty rough section of town. "I hope you're not planning to kick me out of the car down here," Truman joked.

"Don't worry, we're almost there," replied Jerry.

Truman looked out the windows of the car and noticed that they were pulling into a home-less shelter. Already a line of hungry people was gathering at the side door.

"What's the plan? Make me stand in line with those guys to learn some sort of lesson?"

"Not exactly," responded Jerry. "Let's go inside. There is someone I would like you to meet."

They worked their way through the back door and down a narrow hallway. It opened into the spacious kitchen. Lots of workers were busy preparing the shelter's evening meal, and it smelled delicious. . Everyone seemed to know their job and it looked like the food was about to be served. Jerry led Truman to the serving counter and introduced him to Henry, a dapper looking older gentleman.

"Hi, Truman," Henry responded. "Are you here to help out?"

With a glance at Jerry, Truman replied, "Uh, I guess so."

Jerry handed Truman an apron and a set of disposable gloves, "Since we're here, we might as well help. Henry will show you what to do."

For the next hour, Truman ladled mashed potatoes and gravy onto countless plates. As he worked, he listened to Henry and Jerry as they talked to the patrons. They seemed to know most of them by name and even asked many of the people specific questions. And they were quick to introduce themselves to anyone they didn't recognize. Truman smiled at the men and women as he heaped food onto their plates, but inside, he was a little uncomfortable with this situation. He was relieved to see the last guy come up to the line.

"Let's grab ourselves a plate and sit down over there," suggested Henry. "The food's actually pretty good here."

As the three men sat down, Jerry asked, "Are you still unsure why you're here?"

"Well, I'm all for helping out the homeless," said Truman, "but it would have been nice to have a little heads up."

"Sorry about that," Jerry apologized. "I just thought that it might have a more meaningful impact if I was able to catch you off guard. Remember when I told you about my mistakes early on in my youth ministry career?"

"Sure, you said that a well meaning businessman taught you some valuable lessons," Truman answered.

"That's right. And here he is in the flesh," announced Jerry proudly, looking at Henry.

Truman looked at Henry with new eyes. He had assumed that Henry was a volunteer like Jerry. "Where do you work?" asked Truman.

"Well, I used to run the biggest bank in town," Henry said slowly. "Now I run this place." Henry smiled widely.

"Really? That's great. How did you end up here?" asked Truman.

"It's a pretty long and involved story but the short of it is God brought me here. You see, Truman, I thought I had it all figured out. I was making a lot of money. I had a great house and car and was going on great vacations. I thought that I had done all of these things myself. I have been a Christian most of my life and even in that phase of my life I would have told you that I was enjoying God's blessing. The truth was that in my heart I was taking the credit for it and not giving the credit to God."

Truman nodded in acknowledgement. He knew many people with that same problem.

"Then one day I was at a retreat for Christian business leaders. The speaker was talking from the story in Luke 12 about the Rich Fool. The man in that parable was just like me. He looked at all he accomplished and was very proud of his achievements. God worked on me hard through that message and by the end of it, I knew I needed to make a major change. I was worried about what my wife would think. I mean, she would be giving up a lot too. Together we started praying about what we should do and when the opportunity to head up this shelter presented itself, we jumped at it. We know that God has us here for a reason."

Truman was impressed. He didn't meet many people who took their faith as seriously as this man. "Seems like you made some major sacrifices."

"Actually, the opposite is true. I am more alive and effective than I ever have been. The best part about my job is that I now get to rely on God every day. God has taught me more about genuine love and humility through these precious people than I could ever have learned as a CEO."

They continued to talk as they finished their meal. Truman now saw why Jerry was so impressed with Henry. He could listen to this man all day long.

After they had finished cleaning up, Jerry and Truman walked back to Jerry's car. "So, what did you think?" asked Jerry.

"Henry is a great guy," Truman responded. "I feel like I could learn a lot from him."

"I know what you mean. Now you know why I love coming down here. Helping out is a lot of fun, but I also get the benefit of spending some time with Henry. It's a real win-win."

They got in the car and started to make their way home. After a few minutes, Truman asked, "So, what's the next leadership lesson that you wanted to teach me?"

"Actually, I brought you to the master so you could learn from him. Henry has taught me that a leader must be humble in order to be effective. He is a living example of that principle. He gave up a job that came with a lot of power and prestige to work with those who have very little."

"I can see that. I don't know if I have ever met someone who is more humble, gentle, and loving than Henry. And I only spent two hours with him," said Truman.

"What makes Henry a great leader is that he doesn't lead from authority; he leads from influence. It requires a humble leader to lead from a position of influence. As a leader, you have to be willing to let others outshine you, you have to be willing to admit your faults, and you have to listen to the other person's perspective," instructed Jerry.

"Yeah, I can definitely see how that's true. I guess I have always gotten hung up on the fact that humility seems like weakness to me."

"You couldn't be further from the truth, Truman. Humility requires more strength of character than almost any other aspect of leadership. To be humble means being comfortable with who you are, your strengths and your weaknesses, and living in a way that gives God the glory. Humble leaders know what they are good at and do those things well, and they do them for the right reasons. Another word that Jesus used for humility was meekness."

"Okay, I think I get it and I am realizing that humility is missing from my leadership abilities. Just this week I had a run-in with a parent and my response wasn't so great," Truman admitted.

As Truman told Jerry about the interaction with Brad, he could already recognize that Henry or Jerry would have handled that situation differently. He could clearly see how a humble response would have been more effective. "I guess I have a lot to work on when it comes to humility," Truman groaned.

"Don't beat yourself up. God offers His grace to all of us in situations like that. Chalk it up to a learning experience and move on. Though, you might want to revisit that talk with Brad," Jerry suggested.

"Thanks, I think I will."

"Well, here we are," Jerry said as they pulled into the church parking lot. "Before we get together next week, I want you to think through this issue of humility as a leader. Make a list in your journal of where you think pride is getting in your way and confess that to God. Also, I want you to think of three activities that you can do on a regular basis that will remind you to be humble. Now, you know another reason I go to the homeless shelter to help out: it keeps me focused on humility."

Truman got into his car and turned the key. He watched Jerry wave to him and disappear into the church building. He had always thought he understood what humility was until he met these incredibly humble men. He had no doubt that he would be able to fill his journal up tonight.

Leadership Principle:
Embracing Humility

Humility affects many aspects of leadership. Humble leaders are those who are teachable, challenge their followers toward growth, and invite others to share in their mission. Leaders who are not humble find it difficult to develop other leaders around them.

Pride has been the downfall of many leaders. Leaders who are proud are not able to invite others into a relationship of growth and development. Proud leaders often spend more time protecting what is theirs than finding ways to create opportunities for their followers. If you desire to be an effective leader in God's Kingdom, you need to be careful to protect yourself from the pitfalls of a prideful heart.

Again, Jesus gives us a clear example of a leader who is humble. If anyone had reason to be prideful, it was Jesus. Yet, as a leader, He gave up His right to promote Himself. He didn't look for or need the approval and praise of others. The Gospels offer us many examples of Jesus' humility, from His submission to His Father to the love and grace that He showered on those around Him.

John chapter 13 contains the story of a great example of the humility of Christ. Read John 13:1-17 and consider the questions below.

What was Jesus' motivation to do what He did in this passage?

_____

_____

_____

How did these actions affect his followers?

_____

_____

_____

What would have been your response if you were one of the disciples?

_____

_____

_____

Have you ever had a leader show this kind of humility to you? How did you respond?

_____

_____

_____

_____

What is one thing you can do this week to exercise humility as a leader?

_____

_____

_____

_____

Leadership Experience:
The LeaderTreks Spiritual Gifts Inventory

As leaders, we need to be careful not to take humility to its extreme and become self-depre-cating. This does us no good and does not inspire confidence in our followers. It is impor-tant for leaders to realize their strengths as well as their weaknesses. Acknowledging your strengths is not being prideful; it's being honest. It's when you don't recognize the source of those strengths that you can find yourself slipping into pride and arrogance. Godly leaders are quick to recognize how God has gifted them.

One way to discover your gifting is through a spiritual gifts profile. These helpful tools can often open our eyes to ministry and leadership opportunities that we might not have con-sidered on our own. You may have taken a survey like this before. Use the one that we have included here as a refresher to solidify how you think God has gifted you for His service. This tool can help you discover how you are gifted but the real breakthroughs will come as you exercise those gifts in leadership roles.

LeaderTreks

Spiritual Gifts Inventory

Read the following statements carefully. Enter your ratings on the response sheet based on how well the statement describes you, using the following scale:

5   Definitely me
4   Very much like me
3   Somewhat like me
2   Not much like me
1   Definitely not me

		Definitely me	Very much like me	Somewhat like me	Not much like me	Definitely not me
1.	I regularly encourage others to trust God, even when circumstances seem bleak.	5	4	3	2	1
2.	Others see me as caring and sensitive, and open up to me about their feelings.	5	4	3	2	1
3.	I willingly accept responsibility for leading groups that lack direction or motivation.	5	4	3	2	1
4.	I feel compelled to tell others about the inconsistencies I see and their impact.	5	4	3	2	1
5.	I seem better able than most people to sense when others are in need of a lift.	5	4	3	2	1
6.	I find it easy to engage non-believers in conversations about spiritual matters.	5	4	3	2	1
7.	I feel like a partner with the people and organizations I support financially.	5	4	3	2	1
8.	Others often ask me to research topics they want to understand more fully.	5	4	3	2	1
9.	I enjoy guiding and supporting individuals and groups seeking to learn and grow.	5	4	3	2	1
10.	Others see me as highly organized and look for my help in managing projects.	5	4	3	2	1
11.	I find that I am more adventurous and willing to take risks than most people.	5	4	3	2	1
12.	I enjoy analyzing difficult problems and discovering simple, practical solutions.	5	4	3	2	1
13.	I often seem to see matters of injustice or unfairness more clearly than other people.	5	4	3	2	1
14.	I enjoy working unrecognized behind the scenes to support the work of others.	5	4	3	2	1
15.	When I teach, I communicate clearly, and find it easy to engage people in learning.	5	4	3	2	1

		Definitely me	Very much like me	Somewhat like me	Not much like me	Definitely not me
16.	I am confident that God helps us to do great things when we trust Him.	5	4	3	2	1
17.	I am easily moved by others' experience of heartache or suffering.	5	4	3	2	1
18.	I adjust my leadership style to work well with a variety of individuals or groups.	5	4	3	2	1
19.	I seem better able than most people to see the truth of what is really going on.	5	4	3	2	1
20.	Others see me as a positive, optimistic person who can make others feel good.	5	4	3	2	1
21.	I seem to be more concerned than most to share the gospel with non-believers.	5	4	3	2	1
22.	I feel deep satisfaction knowing my giving is making a real difference.	5	4	3	2	1
23.	I enjoy becoming more of an expert on a topic, and sharing my knowledge with others.	5	4	3	2	1
24.	I am more willing than other people to invest time in helping others grow as believers.	5	4	3	2	1
25.	I enjoy being relied upon to organize people and tasks to meet a goal.	5	4	3	2	1
26.	Others see me as a change agent and look to me to lead new undertakings.	5	4	3	2	1
27.	I frequently am able to see potential solutions to problems that others cannot.	5	4	3	2	1
28.	Others see me as a person of strong convictions and willing to speak out.	5	4	3	2	1
29.	I find fulfillment in faithfully performing tasks others see as unglamorous.	5	4	3	2	1
30.	I am confident in my ability to help others learn and apply knowledge and skills.	5	4	3	2	1

		Definitely me	Very much like me	Somewhat like me	Not much like me	Definitely not me
31.	I think I am more confident than most in trusting God, even in the hard times.	5	4	3	2	1
32.	I enjoy helping people that others may regard as undeserving or beyond help.	5	4	3	2	1
33.	I can successfully motivate, guide, and manage others to reach important goals.	5	4	3	2	1
34.	Others see me as insightful, a good judge of people and situations.	5	4	3	2	1
35.	People often seek me out when they are looking for affirmation or encouragement.	5	4	3	2	1
36.	Others see me as being confident in my faith, and ready and willing to share it.	5	4	3	2	1
37.	I give more generously than most people to church and other worthwhile causes.	5	4	3	2	1
38.	I share what I know confidently and clearly, helping others to understand.	5	4	3	2	1
39.	Others see me as a patient, supportive person who brings out the best in others.	5	4	3	2	1
40.	I am skilled at planning, organizing, and managing even complex projects.	5	4	3	2	1
41.	I am always looking for new experiences and love bringing about change.	5	4	3	2	1
42.	When asked to help solve a problem, people usually end up taking my advice.	5	4	3	2	1
43.	I feel a strong sense of responsibility to take a stand for what is right and true.	5	4	3	2	1
44.	I can see how my support with the little things helps others accomplish more.	5	4	3	2	1
45.	I believe I am more motivated to want to help others learn than most people.	5	4	3	2	1

		Definitely me	Very much like me	Somewhat like me	Not much like me	Definitely not me
46.	Others see me as having strong faith, able to provide spiritual encouragement.	5	4	3	2	1
47.	It makes me happy to bring comfort, hope, and joy to people facing difficulties.	5	4	3	2	1
48.	I seem better able than most to help a group work together to achieve its goals.	5	4	3	2	1
49.	I always look below the surface to try to see the truth about people and situations.	5	4	3	2	1
50.	I am drawn to people who are confused or troubled, and try to cheer them up.	5	4	3	2	1
51.	In my relationships with non-believers, I regularly find ways to share my faith.	5	4	3	2	1
52.	It is important to manage my finances well so I can support causes I believe in.	5	4	3	2	1
53.	I like sharing knowledge that improves others' understanding and effectiveness.	5	4	3	2	1
54.	I willingly help others to grow in their faith and to improve their Christian walk.	5	4	3	2	1
55.	I enjoy helping a group to work efficiently and effectively to complete a project.	5	4	3	2	1
56.	I enjoy the challenge of trying new things, despite the unknowns or risks involved.	5	4	3	2	1
57.	I seem to see practical solutions to problems more readily than others.	5	4	3	2	1
58.	I am willing to speak out on matters of right and wrong even if unpopular.	5	4	3	2	1
59.	I seem more willing than most to pitch in wherever I can without being asked.	5	4	3	2	1
60.	Others see me as someone who can make difficult concepts easier to learn.	5	4	3	2	1

		Definitely me	Very much like me	Somewhat like me	Not much like me	Definitely not me
61.	I find it natural and easy to trust God to answer prayer for myself and others.	5	4	3	2	1
62.	I seem more compassionate than most, especially with people who are hurting.	5	4	3	2	1
63.	Others naturally look to me to lead, especially when facing big challenges.	5	4	3	2	1
64.	I can see through phoniness, deception, or error, usually before others are able to.	5	4	3	2	1
65.	I challenge people to look for and affirm the good in themselves and others.	5	4	3	2	1
66.	I like people to know I am a Christian and want them to ask me about my faith.	5	4	3	2	1
67.	I willingly contribute to projects needing my support or people in financial need.	5	4	3	2	1
68.	I think I am better than most people at gathering and sharing information.	5	4	3	2	1
69.	I see the things that hold people back and find ways to help them overcome.	5	4	3	2	1
70.	I think I am more organized than most, better able to manage complex tasks.	5	4	3	2	1
71.	My ability to adapt to new situations makes me comfortable with change.	5	4	3	2	1
72.	Others see me as having a lot of common sense and ask me for advice.	5	4	3	2	1
73.	I am comfortable challenging others to change their thoughts and actions.	5	4	3	2	1
74.	Others see me as always willing to pitch in and do even the smallest routine tasks.	5	4	3	2	1
75.	I enjoy preparing to teach - organizing and planning interesting learning experiences.	5	4	3	2	1

Scoring Guide

Enter your totals from the *Response Sheet* in the appropriate spaces below. Place your score for question #1 in the box marked #1, and so on. After transferring all of your scores, add up the scores for each row and place the total in the column on the right.

Totals

1.	16.	31.	46.	61.	1.
2.	17.	32.	47.	62.	2.
3.	18.	33.	48.	63.	3.
4.	19.	34.	49.	64.	4.
5.	20.	35.	50.	65.	5.
6.	21.	36.	51.	66.	6.
7.	22.	37.	52.	67.	7.
8.	23.	38.	53.	68.	8.
9.	24.	39.	54.	69.	9.
10.	25.	40.	55.	70.	10.
11.	26.	41.	56.	71.	11.
12.	27.	42.	57.	72.	12.
13.	28.	43.	58.	73.	13.
14.	29.	44.	59.	74.	14.
15.	30.	45.	60.	75.	15.

	Gift	Description
1.	**Believing** *(Faith)*	Believing is a special God-given ability to trust God's will and act on it with an unwavering belief in God's concern, presence, and active participation.
2.	**Comforting** *(Mercy)*	Comforting is a special God-given ability to understand and come alongside people who are troubled or suffering, bringing them comfort, insight, and hope.
3.	**Directing** *(Leadership)*	Directing is a special God-given ability to instill vision, motivate, and guide people to work together effectively to achieve worthwhile goals.
4.	**Discerning** *(Discernment)*	Discerning is a special God-given ability to distinguish between truth and error, good and evil, and to show good judgment in matters involving character and relationships.
5.	**Encouraging** *(Exhortation)*	Encouraging is a special God-given ability to affirm, uplift, and restore confidence to individuals who are feeling discouraged or defeated.
6.	**Evangelizing** *(Evangelism)*	Evangelizing is a special God-given ability to effectively communicate the Good News of Jesus Christ to non-believers so they can respond and begin to grow in their faith.
7.	**Giving** *(Contributing)*	Giving is a special God-given ability to contribute cheerfully, generously, and regularly to the church and other important ministries, causes, and people in need.
8.	**Learning** *(Knowledge)*	Learning is a special God-given ability to gather, analyze, and share information appropriately with others, leading to greater understanding and insight.
9.	**Mentoring** *(Pastor/Shepherding)*	Mentoring is a special God-given ability to guide and support individuals or groups as they grow in their faith and in their capacity for ministry.
10.	**Organizing** *(Administration)*	Organizing is a special God-given ability to plan, organize tasks, and follow through so that complex projects are completed efficiently and effectively.
11.	**Pioneering** *(Apostleship)*	Pioneering is a special God-given ability to launch new ventures or lead change, confidently moving forward despite uncertainty or risk.
12.	**Problem-Solving** *(Wisdom)*	Problem-Solving is a special God-given ability to provide practical advice that leads to timely, effective resolution of problems.
13.	**Speaking Out** *(Prophet)*	Speaking Out is a special God-given ability to declare God's truth boldly and publicly for the purpose of correction or instruction.

14.	**Supporting** *(Helps)*	Supporting is a special God-given ability to provide practical, behind-the-scenes help that frees others to accomplish more than they might otherwise be capable of achieving.
15.	**Teaching** *(Teacher)*	Teaching is a special God-given ability to organize and clearly communicate knowledge and skills to others, and to motivate them to master and apply what they are learning.

Review your scores from the scoring sheet. Identify the 2 or 3 spiritual gifts that appear to be your strongest (higher score being stronger) and list these below.

My spiritual gifts may possibly include:

_____

_____

_____

_____

Next, take some time to learn more about these gifts. For each of your strongest gifts, review the gift summaries on the following pages. Take time to understand what each gift is and the unique contribution it enables you to make when you use it wisely. Think of examples where you have been able to use each gift effectively. How did it feel? What results did you achieve? Have you ever experienced any of the problems described in the *Potential Limitation* section of the summary?

_____

_____

_____

_____

Now, think about specific situations in which you could use your unique gifts. Review the sections of the gift summaries entitled *This Gift in Use* and *This Gift in a Team*. Then list 2 or 3 roles or situations where you could effectively utilize your gifts.

Possible ways I can use my spiritual gifts:

_____

_____

_____

Believing
(Faith)

Basic Definition
Believing is a special God-given ability to trust God's will and act on it, with an unwavering belief in God's concern, presence, and active participation.

Unique Leadership Contribution
People with this gift trust God to answer prayer and encourage others to do so, confident in God's help, even in difficult times or in the face of opposition.

This Gift in Scripture
This gift is listed in 1 Corinthians 12:9 where it is usually translated as "faith" or "special faith."

This Gift in Use
People with this gift keep moving forward with confidence, undaunted by obstacles, encouraged by a deeply-rooted belief in God's unending faithfulness and constant care. They are also often the true prayer warriors of the church, lifting its needs to the Lord and seeking His will. When this gift is absent in the church, people can come to doubt God's goodness or His love and concern for His people.

This Gift in a Team
When the going gets tough, people with this gift step up and encourage the rest of the team to keep moving forward, trusting God for strength, guidance, and success.

Typical Strengths
People with this gift tend to be confident, optimistic, prayerful, and reliant on God. By declaring their own trust in God, they encourage others to move forward in faith too.

Potential Pitfalls
People with this gift can become weary and discouraged - or even angry and critical - when others do not share their confidence in God's concern or participation. Using this gift wisely involves remembering and reminding others of the many examples of God's faithfulness in the past, even during the bleakest times.

Comforting
(Mercy)

Basic Definition
Comforting is a special God-given ability to understand and come alongside people who are troubled or suffering, bringing them comfort, insight, and hope.

Unique Leadership Contribution
People with this gift patiently and compassionately help hurting people deal with painful experiences, even those whom others feel are undeserving or beyond help.

This Gift in Scripture
This gift is listed in Romans 12:8 where it is usually translated as "showing mercy" or "showing kindness."

This Gift in Use
People with this gift have a unique capacity for providing timely, practical support to hurting people, seemingly with endless patience, compassion, and joy in their hearts. They respond caringly to others' deepest needs, yet are able to look past their problems and circumstances and see their true worth as if through the eyes of God. When this gift is absent in the church, those who are truly needy will receive too little attention.

This Gift in a Team
In the life of any team there will be times when people need, more than anything, to be comforted by someone who comes alongside even as others pull back.

Typical Strengths
People with this gift tend to be caring, sensitive, and tolerant—natural burden bearers. They sense when people are down, and find ways to be there for them.

Potential Pitfalls
Sometimes, people with this gift become weighed down from carrying the burdens of others. Another problem may be that they may unintentionally enable others to avoid facing their difficulties or making hard choices. Using this gift wisely involves helping hurting people to deal with the underlying causes of their problems and not covering them up.

Directing
(Leadership)

Basic Definition
Directing is a special God-given ability to instill vision, motivate, and guide people to work together effectively to achieve worthwhile goals.

Unique Leadership Contribution
People with this gift willingly take responsibility for directing groups, managing people, and resources effectively, and challenging others to perform at the highest level.

This Gift in Scripture
This gift is listed in Romans 12:8 where it is usually translated as "leadership" or "he who leads."

This Gift in Use
People with this gift help others aspire to and achieve lofty goals. They understand the importance of getting people to perform at their best, both individually and as a group. They relish the opportunity to be in a position of leadership where they can influence the performance of a group that is doing meaningful work. When this gift is absent in the church, people will find themselves falling well short of their potential.

This Gift in a Team
People with this gift are the natural leaders that all teams need to ensure that their efforts are guided by a vision worth pursuing and strategies worth implementing.

Typical Strengths
People with this gift tend to be goal-oriented, decisive, inspiring, and persuasive. They will tend to rise to the top in most groups, emerging naturally as the leader.

Potential Pitfalls
People with this gift need to avoid being over-confident in their own abilities and possibly pushing others away by their perceived arrogance or forcefulness. They can also get stuck in their own ways of doing things, becoming intolerant of others. Using this gift wisely involves building credibility, mutual trust, and support with followers.

Discerning
(Discernment)

Basic Definition
Discerning is a special God-given ability to distinguish between truth and error, good and evil, and to show good judgment in matters involving character and relationships.

Unique Leadership Contribution
People with this gift reliably distinguish between truth and error, good and evil, readily seeing through phoniness and deceit to perceive what is really going on.

This Gift in Scripture
This gift is listed in 1 Corinthians 12:10 where it is usually translated as "distinguishing between spirits" or "discerning of spirits."

This Gift in Use
People with this gift are unusually capable of recognizing inconsistencies in relationships, behavior, motives, teaching, and everyday practices. They quickly perceive the truth about these things, understand the potential consequences, and warn others to be on guard in order to avoid potentially risky situations. When this gift is absent in the church, people fall prey to false teaching or misguided leadership.

This Gift in a Team
At times, a team will find itself in situations where things are not really as they appear and must rely on the finely-tuned perception of someone with this gift to see the truth.

Typical Strengths
People with this gift are insightful, intuitive, and objective. They will often see things differently than others and will strongly defend their views if challenged.

Potential Pitfalls
People with this gift may need to work hard to avoid being seen by others as harsh and inflexible when sharing their insights, especially when their perceptions run counter to what others are thinking. Using this gift wisely involves taking the time to hear others' opinions, and to seek and share evidence that confirms what they think they are seeing.

Encouraging
(Exhortation)

Basic Definition
Encouraging is a special God-given ability to affirm, uplift, and restore confidence to individuals who are feeling discouraged or defeated.

Unique Leadership Contribution
People with this gift sense the needs of others, particularly when they are feeling down, and provide much-appreciated reassurance and cheering up so they can carry on.

This Gift in Scripture
This gift is listed in Romans 12:8 where it is usually translated as "encouraging" or "exhortation."

This Gift in Use
People with this gift readily tune in to others who are in need of a boost. Typically positive and enthusiastic, they sense how others feel and what they need to do to encourage them. Sometimes they challenge or confront, and at other times they cheer up, applaud, or affirm. Whatever the situation, their goal is to help others feel better about themselves. When this gift is absent from a church, people can feel overwhelmed and give up.

This Gift in a Team
Every team needs at least one dedicated cheerleader, and that's a role people with this gift relish. When the going gets tough, they help people stay up and keep moving toward the goal.

Typical Strengths
People with this gift are usually sensitive, positive, and enthusiastic. They see the good in every person, the possibilities in every problem, and the light at the end of the tunnel.

Potential Pitfalls
At times, people with this gift can come across as too simplistic or idealistic. Others don't always appreciate their sunny disposition and unwavering optimism. Using this gift wisely involves acknowledging the reality of the circumstances people are facing and finding ways to offer not only encouragement, but also concrete, practical help.

Evangelizing
(Evangelism)

Basic Definition
Evangelizing is a special God-given ability to effectively communicate the Good News of Jesus Christ to non-believers so they can respond and begin to grow in their faith.

Unique Leadership Contribution
People with this gift find opportunities to build relationships with non-believers, comfortably sharing their faith, and inviting people to decide to follow Christ.

This Gift in Scripture
This gift is listed in Ephesians 4:11 where it is usually translated as "evangelists."

This Gift in Use
People with this gift communicate the Gospel with ease and effectiveness. They seek opportunities to build relationships with non-believers in order to demonstrate the good news of God's love in practical ways, and to get to know people better. This allows them to share their faith in ways that speak directly to the deepest needs of others. When this gift is absent from a church, people are reluctant to witness and outreach to non-believers will be ineffective.

This Gift in a Team
No matter what the primary focus of a team, there will be many opportunities to share the Gospel, and someone with this gift is most likely to recognize these opportunities and respond.

Typical Strengths
People with this gift tend to be social, secure in their faith, open, and candid. They willingly share their faith, doing so naturally and without much fear of rejection or ridicule.

Potential Pitfalls
At times, people with this gift will become discouraged when they are not seeing a response to their evangelistic efforts. Over time, they may become mechanical in their approach, or too aggressive, and turn off non-believers. Using this gift wisely means talking about your relationship with God, and inviting others to begin one of their own.

Giving

(Contributing)

Basic Definition

Giving is a special God-given ability to contribute cheerfully, generously, and regularly to the church and other important ministries, causes, and people in need.

Unique Leadership Contribution

People with this gift manage their personal resources well, contributing as much as possible to people and organizations working to meet needs that are important to them.

This Gift in Scripture

This gift is listed in Romans 12:8 where it is usually translated as "contributing to the needs of others" or "he who gives."

This Gift in Use

People with this gift look for ways to increase their giving to the ministries, causes, and needy individuals they are most committed to supporting. They willingly limit spending on themselves and commit themselves to regular giving. They tend to see themselves as partners with those whose work they support and follow their work closely. When this gift is missing from the church, ministries will lack the resources required to fulfill their mission.

This Gift in a Team

People who are generous givers are often the best individuals to challenge others to do the same, making them a very effective agent for acquiring the resources the team needs.

Typical Strengths

People with this gift tend to be generous, conscientious, prudent, and resourceful. They look beyond their own needs, and see the benefit of meeting the needs of others.

Potential Pitfalls

Sometimes, people with this gift may be tempted to use their resources to pursue a pet project of their own. Or, they can feel unappreciated if their generosity is not adequately recognized. Using this gift wisely involves acknowledging that all we have comes from God and being grateful for the resources we have that we can use for His glory.

Learning
(Knowledge)

Basic Definition
Learning is a special God-given ability to gather, analyze, and share information appropriately with others, leading to greater understanding and insight.

Unique Leadership Contribution
People with this gift research topics of interest to themselves or others, organize their findings systematically, and share what they have learned with others.

This Gift in Scripture
This gift is listed in 1 Corinthians 12:8 where it is usually translated "message of knowledge," "word of knowledge," or "gift of special knowledge."

This Gift in Use
People with this gift are born researchers who love to accumulate and share information. Their unique interest leads them to keep exploring a subject to gain a deeper understanding and more useful information. They enjoy being invited to share their knowledge, helping others quickly gain deeper insight into important matters. When this gift is missing from the church, decisions and plans will be based on inadequate understanding and will eventually fail.

This Gift in a Team
Often people with this gift become a "walking library" of useful information on a wide range of topics crucial to the team's work, as well as the keeper of its learning history.

Typical Strengths
People with this gift tend to be inquisitive, analytical, and proud of their accumulated expertise, with a large appetite for acquiring and sharing information.

Potential Pitfalls
People with this gift need to remember that their latest discovery may not be as exciting to others as to them. They can also fall into the trap of being proud of what they know, even feeling superior to others as a result. The wise use of this gift involves learning to respond to others' self-identified needs for greater understanding in a given area.

Mentoring
(Pastor/Shepherding)

Basic Definition
Mentoring is a special God-given ability to guide and support individuals or groups as they grow in their faith and in their capacity for ministry.

Unique Leadership Contribution
People with this gift are committed to bringing out the best in others, patiently but firmly nurturing them in their development as whole persons, often on a long-term basis.

This Gift in Scripture
This gift is listed in Ephesians 4:11 where it is usually translated as "pastors."

This Gift in Use
People with this gift willingly accept responsibility for guiding and protecting people who they believe God has entrusted to their care. They identify others' strengths and limitations, and look for timely opportunities to challenge them to grow. Their long-term concern for people makes them highly trusted advisors and coaches. When this gift is missing from the church, people will remain weak in their faith and their Christian walk.

This Gift in a Team
Often people with this gift support a team by supporting its members in an ongoing process of personal and ministry development, both as individuals and as a group.

Typical Strengths
People with this gift tend to be nurturing, growth-minded, and discipleship-oriented. They will look for ways to maximize each person's growth and contribution.

Potential Pitfalls
People with this gift need to be careful about viewing certain people as projects. They may also have difficulty saying no, which can lead to burn-out. Using this gift wisely involves recognizing and maintaining appropriate boundaries, developing healthy relationships that avoid creating dependency between or among those involved.

Organizing
(Administration)

Basic Definition
Organizing is a special God-given ability to plan, organize tasks, and follow through so that complex projects are completed efficiently and effectively.

Unique Leadership Contribution
People with this gift ensure the success of a project by clarifying goals, developing detailed plans, delegating tasks, monitoring performance, and managing follow-through.

This Gift in Scripture
This gift is listed in 1 Corinthians 12:28 where it is usually translated as "administration," "governments," or "those who can get others to work together."

This Gift in Use
People with this gift have the capacity to coordinate people, tasks, and resources even in very complex circumstances. Working within the context of the project's goals, they focus on both doing the right things and doing things right. They know how to bring order out of chaos in organizations, always able to see how everything fits together. When this gift is missing from the church, people will become frustrated by confusion, waste, and the inability to get things done.

This Gift in a Team
With so many tasks and people to manage, complexity is a fact of life for most teams. People with this gift develop the systems, processes, and plans to make it all work.

Typical Strengths
People with this gift tend to be highly-organized, thorough, clear-thinking, and conscientious. They are comfortable with detail and strive for order and harmony.

Potential Pitfalls
People with this gift must be careful not to frustrate other leaders who don't share their enthusiasm for thoroughness and detail. Also, when things aren't going well, they can sometimes seem to be "using people" simply to accomplish tasks. Using this gift wisely involves balancing task requirements and deadlines with people's needs and feelings.

Pioneering
(Apostleship)

Basic Definition
Pioneering is a special God-given ability to launch new ventures or lead change, confidently moving forward despite uncertainty or risk.

Unique Leadership Contribution
People with this gift lead the way in spearheading change, testing out new ideas, or leading innovation, often producing breakthroughs in growth or effectiveness.

This Gift in Scripture
This gift is listed in 1 Corinthians 12:28 and Ephesians 4:11 where it is usually translated as "apostles."

This Gift in Use
People with this gift have little fear of the unknown, and an appetite for adventure and even risk. They look for opportunities for growth and change, seeking to move beyond the status quo. Where others get anxious, they get excited. Where others see obstacles, they see opportunities. They always look forward to the next challenge. When this gift is missing from the church, people will find it very difficult to bring about change or start something new.

This Gift in a Team
Even high performing teams can sometimes find themselves in a rut. It takes someone with this gift to stir things up, keep looking ahead, and push for much-needed changes.

Typical Strengths
People with this gift tend to be adventurous, risk-taking, adaptable, and confident. Being natural entrepreneurs, they have a make-it-happen approach to the future.

Potential Pitfalls
At times, people with this gift will move too quickly and get ahead of others. They may find themselves disconnected from the supporters they need, sometimes even alienating them. Using this gift wisely involves engaging others in creating a shared vision and in making plans to get there.

Problem-Solving
(Wisdom)

Basic Definition
Problem-Solving is a special God-given ability to provide practical advice that leads to timely, effective resolution of problems.

Unique Leadership Contribution
People with this gift can often identify simple, practical solutions to problems, helping others find ways to get unstuck and confidently move forward toward their goals.

This Gift in Scripture
This gift is listed in 1 Corinthians 12:8 where it is usually translated as "message of wisdom," "word of wisdom," or "the ability to give wise advice."

This Gift in Use
People with this gift see solutions where others may only see roadblocks. They seem to be able to cut through confusion and conflict and see how to overcome obstacles. They are good at figuring out the best action to take in a given situation. Blessed with an uncommon amount of common sense, they offer practical advice that others willingly follow. When this gift is missing from the church, people may repeat past mistakes or continue doing things the hard way.

This Gift in a Team
Every team runs into problems and needs someone who can offer practical advice to get the team back on track as well as helping the team avoid getting bogged down in the first place.

Typical Strengths
People with this gift will tend to be logical, sensible, observant, and highly practical. They will see options others miss and carefully choose the most effective way forward.

Potential Pitfalls
People with this gift may be tempted to hold back from sharing their insights until someone invites them to do so, perhaps because they have learned that others are not always open to advice. Using this gift wisely involves learning how to share important insights and suggestions in ways that others can understand and embrace them.

Speaking Out
(Prophet)

Basic Definition
Speaking Out is a special God-given ability to declare God's truth boldly and publicly for the purpose of correction or instruction.

Unique Leadership Contribution
People with this gift challenge others to change their behavior by speaking out clearly and convincingly about right and wrong, even where it may be unpopular.

This Gift in Scripture
This gift is listed in Romans 12:6, 1 Corinthians 12:10, 28, and Ephesians 4:11 where it is usually translated as "prophesying," "prophets," or "ability to prophesy."

This Gift in Use
People with this gift are especially attuned both to God's principles and to what is really going on in the world. They look for the right time and place to share what they feel must be said to influence others. They tend to see issues that others fail to see and feel compelled to speak out. When this gift is missing from the church, people can lose touch with God's heart and his will.

This Gift in a Team
Often people with this gift support a team by serving as a kind of "moral compass," challenging others to live up to biblical standards of right and wrong.

Typical Strengths
People with this gift will tend to be individualistic, opinionated, outspoken, and determined. They will see situations and issues in very clear, black-and-white terms.

Potential Pitfalls
At times, people with this gift will be difficult to be around because of their strong need to speak out, which may be perceived as overly judgmental and critical of others. Using this gift wisely involves being compassionate toward others and having a genuine desire to motivate others to change rather than a need simply to point out where they arewrong.

Supporting
(Helps)

Basic Definition
Supporting is a special God-given ability to provide practical, behind-the-scenes help that frees others to accomplish more than they might otherwise be capable of achieving.

Unique Leadership Contribution
People with this gift usually like to work behind the scenes, supporting the work of others, cheerfully finding and doing small things that need doing, often without being asked.

This Gift in Scripture
This gift is listed in Romans 12:7 and 1 Corinthians 12:28 where it is usually translated as "helps," "serving," "ministry," "forms of assistance," or "those able to help others."

This Gift in Use
People with this gift take pride in doing well the seemingly small tasks others sometimes consider mundane or routine. They appreciate how their faithful assistance with these tasks pays off by freeing others to focus their attention on "higher level" tasks and enables them to use their gifts more fully. When this gift is missing from the church, leaders can become bogged down by details or worn out from trying to do everything alone.

This Gift in a Team
No one gets to do the glamorous work all of the time, but those with this gift willingly take on the more routine tasks, making it possible for high-performing teams to excel.

Typical Strengths
People with this gift tend to be flexible, easy-going, dependable, and humble. They take pride in serving others faithfully without concern for recognition or honor.

Potential Pitfalls
People with this gift often find it difficult to say no, causing them to over-commit, which leads to a loss of balance in their lives. Some also come to depend on what they do for others for their self-worth. Using this gift wisely involves recognizing that God values people for who they are, not what they do, and by maintaining a healthy, balanced life.

Teaching
(Teacher)

Basic Definition
Teaching is a special God-given ability to organize and clearly communicate knowledge and skills to others, and to motivate them to master and apply what they are learning.

Unique Leadership Contribution
People with this gift identify the knowledge and skills others need to learn, and use creative approaches to help them learn willingly and effectively.

This Gift in Scripture
This gift is listed in Romans 12:7, 1 Corinthians 12:28, and Ephesians 4:11 where it is usually translated as "teaching" or "teacher."

This Gift in Use
People with this gift focus on helping others develop their knowledge and skill, including their knowledge of Christian principles. They begin by understanding the learning needs of others, and then look for teachable moments to engage people in creative, enjoyable learning activities that lead to knowledge and skill improvement. When this gift is missing from the church, people will not grow in depth of faith or capacity for ministry.

This Gift in a Team
Often people with this gift have the best feel for the strengths and limitations of the team. They often can tell what others need to learn and how to help them learn it.

Typical Strengths
People with this gift will usually be skilled at organizing ideas, creative, and enthusiastic. They have a special knack for making difficult concepts easier to learn.

Potential Pitfalls
The most common shortcoming of people with this gift is their tendency to over-teach, presenting too much content and not enough opportunity for reflection, review, and experimenting with application. Using this gift wisely involves continually "checking in" with the learners and adjusting to their motivation, pace, and learning style.

Application:

Any discussion of humility should lead to application. None of us are as humble as we should be. Make an action plan for you to continue to work on being a humble leader. Work through these questions.

Make a list of any areas of your life about which you are prideful. By writing them down you will be able to better recognize them. Confess these things to God.

_____

_____

_____

_____

_____

What are 2-3 activities that you can engage in on a regular basis that will help keep you humble?

_____

_____

_____

_____

Do you know a leader who is humble? Make a connection with that person and ask them questions about how they maintain humility as a leader.

CHAPTER FOUR

BECOMING A LEADER OF LEADERS

Chapter 4

The past several weeks had been revolutionary for Truman. As he sat at his desk and read through the pages of his leadership journal, he was beginning to realize how far he had come. The best part for him was that ministry was becoming fun again. For the first time in months, he looked forward to coming to the office, meeting with students, and chatting with parents.

He had intentionally focused on developing his humility and integrity as a leader. Just last Sunday he was able to find Brad, the parent who had given Truman a piece of his mind, and apologize to him. Brad accepted the apology and even expressed remorse for his part in the exchange. Truman felt good about restoring that relationship. As other opportunities came up, Truman made it a point to be a leader who was willing to do the hard things and be humble toward others.

His new attitude was already making a difference. Students were more responsive during youth group events. Critical relationships in Truman's life were being strengthened. And the youth ministry seemed to be regaining momentum. Even though things were going well, a nagging sense of doubt hid in the back of Truman's mind. He could see the improvements but he also sensed something was missing.

Truman stared hard at the wall on the other side of the office as he tried to sort things out in his mind. He thought through the last few weeks, all the meetings with students, youth group events, and volunteer team meetings. As he worked the situation over in his mind, he started to realize that he was doing everything himself. He was the only one leading. He had great volunteers and capable students, but no one was assuming a leadership role. He needed to find a way to get other leaders involved and help them take ownership.

He scribbled some more notes into his leadership journal and glanced at his watch. He was meeting Jerry at the coffee shop in twenty minutes.

Truman hustled into the coffee shop, not surprised to see Jerry already occupying his usual booth. Truman skipped the caffeine and went straight over to Jerry. He sat down opposite of his mentor and asked, "How's it going?"

"I'm doing better than I deserve," said Jerry. "You look especially lively today. What's going on in your world?"

"Well, I've been doing some self-evaluation this morning."

"That's an excellent sign of good leadership," Jerry interrupted.

"Well, it's all because of this leadership journal," Truman responded. "I've really enjoyed it and I think that I may have figured out what is still missing in my youth ministry."

"Well, don't keep me in suspense," Jerry quipped.

"I'm sure this would have been obvious to you, but I noticed something that might be pretty big. I've been trying to invest in myself so I can become a better leader. I agree with what you said to me earlier that the most important investment in my ministry will be what I do personally to become a better leader."

"So, how's it going? Do you see ways that you are becoming a better leader?" asked Jerry.

"Sure, lots of ways. The students seem more engaged, the parents are happier, and my senior pastor gave me a little pep talk this week about all the good stuff he has been hearing. In spite of all that, I noticed something's still missing. When I looked hard at my ministry this morning I realized that I'm the only one leading. It seems that there are other capable people, but none of them are stepping up and taking leadership responsibility," said Truman.

"Let me ask you a question, Truman. Have you ever been on a team where there were multiple people who were willing to stand up and lead?" Jerry asked.

That question forced Truman to pause. First he thought about his experiences in high school and college sports. Then he thought of the summer he spent working at the summer camp he had attended as a child. The staff at camp was able to work together very well. There had been a director who divided the leadership roles based on the strengths of the staff, and he let each staff member lead in the way that seemed best to them. Everyone there had worked hard because they didn't want to let their friends down. So Truman related this experience to Jerry.

"Sounds like your camp director was a great leader," commented Jerry. "It's clear that he understood the next leadership principle I want to teach you. What your director was for you and what you need to become for your ministry is a leader who models leadership for one's followers and then releases them to be leaders themselves. It can be summed up in the phrase *become a leader of leaders*."

"Yeah, that's a good way to describe my camp director," agreed Truman. "He was a man of humility and integrity, like we've already talked about. He was also a man who was able to get out of the way and let others lead. He was very good at developing other leaders."

"In fact," said Jerry, "this issue might be the best measure of the effectiveness of a leader. As you have already discovered, there is only so much that you can do to lead your ministry. Sooner or later you will come to the end of your own resources. What you do at that critical juncture is of vital importance."

"I feel like I might already be there," said Truman quietly.

"Of course you are. Every leader finds themselves at the end of their means at one point or another. Ineffective leaders seem to just try harder to accomplish everything on their own. They end up doing things they are not gifted in doing, tasks that are not in their strengths areas. This only leads to frustration and burnout."

"You're preaching to the choir here," Truman joked. "I get the problem, but what's the solution?"

"Well, the solution is beautifully simple in theory but complex in implementation," Jerry said. "You have to find a way to release others in leadership just like your camp director did. Becoming a good leader of leaders involves three critical elements: evaluation, mentoring, and trust."

Truman opened his leadership journal and started taking notes. "Tell me more."

"It all starts with the first skill of evaluation. As a leader you need to be constantly evaluating your team to see how you can continue to challenge each of your volunteers and student leaders. This requires judgment and understanding as you set development goals for the key players in your ministry. A great question to ask is 'What is this person's greatest need?' If you can answer that question you will be able to set valuable goals for that individual."

Truman thought about this for a second. "That seems a little like 'playing God.' Isn't it kind of presumptuous to determine for other people how they should grow as a leader?"

"It can seem like that on the surface," Jerry admitted, "but the truth is, every great leader in your life has done this for you. You just might not have been aware of it. In fact, I have been setting development goals for you since I met you. That's why we are having this conversation now. If I didn't prayerfully consider how I could help you grow, I would be wasting your time as well as my own."

"Yeah, I guess that makes sense. I guess I need to take the leadership responsibility in these relationships that God has brought into my life."

"Exactly. It's your job to evaluate what will help your people continue to grow," said Jerry.

"Now let's talk about the next step. After you set development goals for your people, you need to mentor them as they take those first steps in their new leadership role. I'm not talking about the kind of mentoring that has become a meaningless buzz word in today's Christian culture. Often that type of mentoring is focused only on spending relational time together. While time together is important, it doesn't bring about lasting change. Mentoring must go deeper than that."

"What do you mean?"

"What I call *leadership mentoring* is an intentional relationship between a mentor and their follower. It requires the mentor to empower the follower with all the skills and authority needed to take the next leadership risk. The mentor must walk alongside the leader and provide constructive feedback and support as needed. Ultimately, the mentor must release the leader to find their own path."

"Sounds like a good plan," Truman agreed. "But how does one do that?"

"It starts with a commitment to encourage your followers toward the goals that you have set for them. Many leaders fail to take this mentoring risk for a number of reasons. For example, maybe they are afraid to give up control or they're worried their followers will eclipse them as leaders. But good leaders must be willing to correct followers as they need it and support them in their endeavors."

"OK, that's definitely something I can work on. Tell me about the final skill needed to become a leader of leaders."

"The last step is one of the most difficult and most important, and it's what separates good leaders from legendary leaders." Jerry paused to take a breath. "This crucial skill is the ability of a leader to place trust in their followers. Many leaders pay lip service to delegation. But often they are only willing to delegate the things they don't care about. Or they might attempt to rescue the young leader if they think the plan is about to fail. It doesn't take long for your followers to sense these things, and when they do, those leaders will be unwilling to take any risks. How are you at trusting the other leaders in your ministry?"

Truman stared at the table with a guilty look on his face. He thought about the last couple of weeks and realized that he hadn't been trusting his followers much at all. The only jobs his adult volunteers were actually doing were the ones he didn't like. And he had intervened when he thought his students weren't going to come through with the plans for the outreach event.

"But how can I let an event or activity fail if I am the one responsible for it?" asked Truman.

"I don't think the church leadership would be too happy if I did that."

"That is a valid point," agreed Jerry. "But think about the goals you have for your ministry. Are you more interested in running flawless events or empowering adults and students with ownership and leadership in your ministry? Is it better to attain perfection or to help people grow? When you are in charge, do all of the events go perfectly?"

"OK, OK, I get it," Truman responded as he held up his hands. "I make mistakes and I need to make room for other people to make mistakes. I know I've learned from my failures, so I guess I need to help my future leaders learn the same way."

"That's right, Truman. Now you are getting it. But it wouldn't hurt if you explained this approach to the church leadership. If they are in the loop they are often much more forgiving of ministry failures."

"Yeah, I've been working on that." Truman said. "Once again, you have given me a lot to think about."

"Let me leave you with one last thought. The best leaders place people in their areas of strength. They make goals for development for people in a way that allows them to utilize their natural skills and abilities. As a leader, you must first understand your own strengths if you want to help your people discover their strengths as well," said Jerry.

As their conversation came to a close, Truman realized he had been missing a major component of what it meant to be a leader. He knew that he needed to become intentional about developing the leaders around him. Jerry had given him a new goal, and it would require him to learn a whole new set of skills as a leader.

Truman left the coffee shop ready to implement a new leadership development plan for his student ministry. He recognized the kind of difference this could make and he was excited to see what would happen.

Leadership Principle:
Becoming a Leader of Leaders

Throughout history, all truly effective leaders have understood how to be a leader of leaders. Learning this skill is an essential. At the same time, to become a proficient leader of leaders requires learning a whole new set of skills. Becoming a leader who can empower others to lead is not easy, but it is well worth it.

The three crucial skills of evaluation, mentoring, and trust are the bedrock skills you must develop in order to grow other leaders. Evaluation comes first. This skill requires a critical eye and the ability to help new leaders discover what their next leadership step is. You can start by asking the question, "What is this person's greatest need?" This will help you understand how to help this future leader grow. The next necessary skill is the ability to mentor. This means more than just spending time together. It is an intentional process that provides the new leader with feedback on how they are doing and ways they can improve. The final skill is placing trust in this new leader. Trust allows the new leader room to succeed or fail and ultimately to grow. Without trust, you will have a difficult time letting the new leader take the reins of leadership.

As you can see, becoming a leader of leaders requires an intentional focus on knowing and developing your own strengths as a leader. Again, Jesus provides us a great leadership example. He spent much of his ministry time developing a core group of men and women who He would trust to carry on His mission. His goal was to create a movement of people who would proclaim God's love to the world. Jesus took advantage of many opportunities to empower His followers throughout the Gospels. To see an example of how Jesus empowered his followers, read Matthew 10:1-20. Then answer the following questions:

How would you characterize the tone of Jesus' talk with His disciples?

_____

_____

What do you think was going through the minds of the disciples as they thought about what Jesus said?

_____

_____

Have you ever felt like the disciples felt here?

_____

_____

How can you emulate Jesus' example in your ministry?

_____

_____

Leadership Experience:
The LeaderTreks Leadership Type Assessment

Becoming a leader of leaders requires a new understanding of leadership in a whole new way. Leaders must not only understand their strengths but also recognize the leadership strengths of those around them. There is a role for every type of leader on your team. By understanding each person's leadership strengths, you can find the role that fits them.

This assessment will provide a common perspective from which to evaluate yourself and your other team members. Through some simple questions you will discover if you are a doer, thinker, relater, or mover. Like all assessments, this one is not foolproof. It can, however, underscore the ways in which you often lead, and give you a picture of what your obstacles may be to becoming a leader of leaders.

LeaderTreks

Leadership Type Assessment

A team is a group of people who have come together for a purpose. The reasons for forming a team may vary widely, but the ingredients for a good team are the same. Every team needs to get along, to get something done, to develop creative solutions, and to accomplish the goal. These are the key ingredients for any team, but team leaders tend not to pay equal attention to all of the ingredients. In fact, each of us tends to pay attention primarily to only one of the ingredients. The team ingredient you care most about and pay attention to defines your leadership type.

There are four main leadership types. This tool will help you identify your primary type and recognize the importance and contribution of all the types. You will be a better team leader and team member when you become aware of your leadership type and recognize the leadership type of others.

Scoring Instructions
Following are ten statements. Complete each statement by selecting the answer that best describes you. Don't worry if your answers seem inconsistent. Treat each statement as a unique situation. Select only one response for each statement. Mark the box on the right to indicate your answer.

Response Sheet
When you've finished answering each section, transfer your answers to the response chart to discover your leadership type. Circle the letter corresponding to the answers you marked for each question. Then total your score at the bottom of each column.

1. When I'm a part of a work group...
   a. I would rather focus on getting the work done
   b. I would rather be responsible for planning and problem-solving
   c. I would rather focus on relationships
   d. I would rather be responsible for the team as a whole

1.
☐ a
☐ b
☐ c
☐ d

2. I am the kind of person who prefers...
   a. Getting to know the other people on a project
   b. Getting other people to work on a project
   c. Working on each step of a project
   d. Planning a project

2.
☐ a
☐ b
☐ c
☐ d

3. People sometimes tell me that I am...
   a. Good at thinking ahead
   b. Good at organizing things
   c. Good at taking charge
   d. Good at listening and befriending

3.
☐ a
☐ b
☐ c
☐ d

4. When helping with a long and boring task...
   a. I would tend to make sure everyone was involved and helping
   b. I would tend to talk with others as we worked
   c. I would tend to think about other ways to do our work
   d. I would tend to pitch in right away and do my part

4.
☐ a
☐ b
☐ c
☐ d

5. I like it when other people...
   a. Tell me I'm doing good work
   b. Tell me I'm creative
   c. Tell me I know how to make things happen
   d. Tell me they appreciate me as a person

5.
☐ a
☐ b
☐ c
☐ d

6. When I encounter a problem or obstacle, I like to...
   a. Bring others together to work it out
   b. Take quick action and see what happens
   c. Talk it through with another person for clarity
   d. Take some time to think about it and generate options

6.
☐ a
☐ b
☐ c
☐ d

7. I consider myself to be more...
    a. Idea oriented
    b. People oriented
    c. Task oriented
    d. Goal oriented
	7.
	☐ a
	☐ b
	☐ c
	☐ d

8. Other people have told me I tend to be good at...
    a. Completing projects
    b. Being in charge
    c. Coming up with new ideas
    d. Meeting new people
	8.
	☐ a
	☐ b
	☐ c
	☐ d

9. What bothers me is when...
    a. People aren't friendly
    b. People don't finish their work
    c. People won't take risks
    d. People don't use their head
	9.
	☐ a
	☐ b
	☐ c
	☐ d

10. Here is the most important outcome to me...
    a. I just want the team to win or reach the goal
    b. I just want team members to grow
    c. I just want teammates to get along
    d. I just want the team to get it right
	10.
	☐ a
	☐ b
	☐ c
	☐ d

Question	Doer	Thinker	Relater	Mover
1	A	B	C	D
2	C	D	A	B
3	B	A	D	C
4	D	C	B	A
5	A	B	D	C
6	B	D	C	A
7	C	A	B	D
8	A	C	D	B
9	B	D	A	C
10	D	B	C	A
Total				

Your highest total score is your primary leadership type. Write the name of your leadership type in the space below. If another type scored a close second, write the name of that type as your supporting type. If no other type scored close, then leave that space blank.

My primary leadership type: _____

My supporting leadership type (if any): _____

Growth Strategies

What Do the Leadership Types Mean?

The four leadership types are Doer, Thinker, Relater, and Mover. Each type shows a primary concern about one of the ingredients for a good team: getting something done, developing solutions, getting along, and accomplishing the goal.

Doers are primarily concerned about the tasks to be accomplished by the team. They like to focus on the task at hand, make checklists, get things organized, correct errors, and hit deadlines. Doers want the team to get it right.

Thinkers are primarily concerned about generating new ideas and solving team problems. They like to gather information, analyze a situation, brainstorm new ideas, develop plans, be creative, and get all the pieces working together. Thinkers want the team to develop creative solutions.

Relaters are primarily concerned about people and team relationships. They like to get to know the other team members, build relationships, encourage others, be a good listener, and be supportive. Relaters want the team members to get along.

Movers are primarily concerned about achieving goals and getting the team from here to there. Movers like to accept challenges, set goals, get others involved, make decisions, take appropriate risks, and persevere over difficulties. Movers want the team to win.

Every team needs to get along, to get something done, to develop solutions, and to accomplish the goal. Each leadership type addresses one of these four important ingredients. Next, you will compare all four types to confirm your score and find ways to improve the way you lead a team.

Leadership Type Grid

Here is a comparison of the four leadership types. Read through all of the descriptions to discover how people behave like you or unlike you as they lead or contribute to a team. Using a highlighter or pen, mark all of the tendencies that describe you. Then focus on your primary type and mark one or two steps you can take to become a more effective team member or team leader.

Doer		Thinker	
Concerned primarily about tasks to be accomplished by the team		Concerned primarily about generating new ideas and solving team problems	
Tendencies in a team setting may include:	*To be more effective as a team leader:*	*Tendencies in a team setting may include:*	*To be more effective as a team leader:*
• Focusing on the task at hand • Organizing the work of others • Making checklists • Starting and completing projects • Improving the process • Setting and meeting deadlines • Correcting errors • Wanting to get the work done • Wanting the team to get it right	• Be sensitive to needs of others • Avoid being over controlling • Share the workload • Show respect for team members • Show appreciation for efforts of others • Be willing to try new procedures • Avoid attitude of using people • Commit to building relationships	• Thinking ahead • Being creative • Gathering information • Analyzing a situation • Talking about issues in the group • Brainstorming new ideas • Developing plans • Getting pieces to work together • Wanting to solve team problems	• Avoid needing to be right all the time • Avoid bogging down in detail • Don't criticize other team members • Show respect for people • Don't be a loner • Be willing to take responsibility • Be more positive and optimistic • Commit to being a part of the team

Relater		Mover	
Concerned primarily about people and team relationships		Concerned primarily about goals and getting the team from here to there	
Tendencies in a team setting may include:	*To be more effective as a team leader:*	*Tendencies in a team setting may include:*	*To be more effective as a team leader:*
• Building relationships • Being supportive and loyal • Showing appreciation • Encouraging others • Acknowledging someone's effort • Being a good listener • Being agreeable • Sticking with the team • Wanting people to get along	• Be aware of what needs to be done • Pay attention to the schedule • Be willing to share your ideas • Be flexible and open to change • Ask for help in prioritizing work • Avoid withdrawing when people disagree • Commit to reaching team goals	• Setting goals • Accepting challenges • Taking charge • Wanting immediate results • Getting others involved • Making quick decisions • Taking appropriate risks • Persevering over difficulties • Wanting the team to win	• Be open to ideas of others • Get the facts and details • Avoid unnecessary risks • Be patient with team members • Avoid being demanding or bossy • Strive to remain humble • Respect authorities over you • Commit to sharing leadership

Ministry Match

For further application, use this chart as a guide for how well your leadership type matches these typical ministry responsibilities.

Ministry Responsibility	Doer	Thinker	Relater	Mover
Acting, singing, or playing music	Low	High	Low	Medium
Advising others on personal finances	High	Low	Low	Medium
Arranging social events	Medium	Low	High	Low
Building relationships	Low	Low	High	Low
Caring for hurting people	Low	Low	High	Low
Catering or cooking	Medium	Low	High	Low
Chairing meetings	Low	Low	Medium	High
Coaching a team	Low	Low	Medium	High
Constructing or building	High	Medium	Low	Low
Coordinating a group	High	Low	High	Medium
Counseling a needy person	Low	Low	High	Low
Developing teaching materials	Low	High	Low	Low
Directing a performance	Low	Medium	Low	High
Discipling others in their faith	Medium	High	Medium	Low
Doing routine tasks behind the scenes	High	Low	Low	Low
Doing secretarial or clerical work	High	Low	Medium	Low
Drawing or designing	Low	High	Low	Low
Encouraging people in need	Low	Low	High	Low
Entertaining at home	Low	Medium	High	Low
Evaluating programs	Medium	High	Low	Low
Fixing or repairing things	High	Low	Low	Low
Fundraising	Low	Low	Low	High
Gathering and distributing information	High	High	Low	Low
Leading a discussion	Low	High	Medium	Low
Maintaining or cleaning	High	Low	Low	Low
Making crafts or decorations	High	High	Medium	Low

Ministry Responsibility	Doer	Thinker	Relater	Mover
Nurturing a small group	Low	Medium	High	Low
Operating equipment or vehicles	High	Low	Low	Low
Organizing a project or event	High	Low	Medium	Low
Overseeing a program	Low	Medium	Low	High
Pioneering a new ministry	Low	Low	Low	High
Planning and envisioning	Low	Medium	Low	High
Promoting a program or project	Low	Low	Low	High
Recruiting volunteers	Low	Low	Medium	High
Researching or studying	Low	High	Low	Low
Resolving conflicts	Low	Low	Low	High
Speaking or preaching	Low	Medium	Low	High
Supervising others	Low	Low	High	High
Teaching a class	Low	High	Medium	Low
Training others	Medium	High	Low	Low
Tutoring individuals	Medium	High	High	Low
Visiting with the sick or elderly	Low	Low	High	Low
Welcoming people	Low	Low	High	Low
Witnessing	Low	Low	Medium	High
Writing or editing	Low	High	Low	Low

Application

Now it's time for you to think about what you need to do to become a leader who inspires and empowers the leaders around you. Think about your own leadership position and answer the following questions:.

List three leaders in your ministry (adults or students). What is their greatest need? What can you do this week to help them take the next leadership risk?

_____

_____

_____

_____

_____

_____

_____

Is there anything about your leadership style that might be keeping people from taking leadership risks in your ministry? How could you change those things?

_____

_____

_____

_____

_____

_____

Commit to speaking to another leader whom you respect as a leader of leaders this week. Ask them to mentor you in this process of becoming an empowering leader.

CHAPTER FIVE

FOCUSING ON MISSION:
BURDEN+PASSION+VISION=MISSION

Chapter 5

Truman slumped into his favorite chair at home, exhausted but satisfied. The last five or six weeks of ministry had been especially tiring, but at the same time he was more motivated than ever to pursue his calling. Working hard on his leadership skills had really started to pay off. While the impact in his ministry was undeniable, the biggest change had come in his own life. His inner life was improving. He was also starting to see new ways to influence the people around him. For the first time in a long time he was growing as a leader and so were others around him. It was exciting.

As he sat in the living room and surfed the channels on the TV, Truman's mind was elsewhere. He was starting to see new growth in his group, but could he sustain it? What was the next step for him as a leader? What would it take to help his students grow deeper in their relationship with Christ? These uncertainties plagued his thoughts. More than anything, Truman wanted to see his ministry continue to grow and thrive.

He had come to value this new direction more than he first realized. Now he needed to find a way to continue what he had started. Maybe Jerry had some wisdom to shed on this situation. Truman realized now the great gift that Jerry had given him these past weeks; having a mentor had helped Truman recognize the power of mentoring relationships. Jerry will help me figure out how to maintain this momentum, Truman thought to himself. Truman was looking forward to seeing his mentor in the morning.

The next morning found Truman digging through the pile of unused sporting equipment in the corner of the garage. Jerry had invited him to go fishing and he needed to find his old fishing pole. Truman was surprised at his growing excitement as he realized how anxious he was to try fishing again. He loved to be outside and it would be good to spend some uninterrupted time with Jerry. He finally found the old rod along with the small tackle box filled with odds and ends that his grandfather had given him.

Truman pulled into the parking lot, grabbed his gear, and headed toward the dock. He could see that Jerry already had the boat in the water and was rigging his fishing rod as he sat in the back of the boat next to the small outboard motor. "Hey, this is a nice little boat," Truman said as he tossed his stuff in the front and jumped lightly into the boat.

"Thanks. It used to belong to my dad but he gave it to me after he quit fishing," responded Jerry. "I still take him out once in a while."

"What are we fishing for today?"

"Well, since it's spring, I know some coves where we can find a few bluegills in the shallow water. I was hoping to get a few for the frying pan. Have you ever had fresh pan fish fried in lemon and garlic? It's unbelievable," Jerry said with a grin on his face.

The two men slowly motored away from the dock, enjoying the warm spring sunshine. "This old motor won't move us too fast but it will give us a chance to talk. How have things been going for you lately, Truman?"

"Actually, better than I deserve," Truman said, stealing a line from his mentor. "I was just thinking last night about all the growth I have seen lately in my own life and in the lives of my students. It has been exciting. My adult volunteers have started taking more responsibility lately, and I have been working hard to help them discover their passions and strengths. I have seen them grow in their own leadership abilities as they discover what it is they love to do. At church this past weekend, one of my volunteers told me about a rewarding conversation she had with a student in our ministry. She wouldn't have taken that risk if I wasn't willing to challenge her."

"That's great. What else is going well?"

"I have also noticed that my attitude towards people is changing and it is having a positive effect on my relationships. Students have been opening up to me more now that I'm trying to ask deeper questions. Even parents who were out to get me before are coming around. I have been trying to be humble and consistent in my leadership and I think it's making a difference," Truman said with a beaming smile.

Jerry smiled back at his protégée. "I've seen the changes too, Truman. You are much more willing to learn and grow than when I first met you. Now, let me ask you another question: what do you think has made the difference?"

The conversation in the boat lulled as Truman contemplated that question. "That's a great question. I wish I had a good answer. If you really pressed me on it I would have to say that I think the change has been a result of what you have taught me. What I'm really afraid of is that I won't be able to continue to grow myself and others in this same way." Truman's face took on a serious look as Jerry piloted into the secluded cove.

The boat drifted to a stop and Jerry killed the engine. The quiet that settled over them was almost palpable. Jerry thought for a few moments and then said, "I'm really glad to hear you thinking like this Truman. That is ultimately one of the biggest leadership questions any of us face. How do you keep growing yourself and those around you? It's a tough question. One that I have struggled with myself as a leader. After years of thinking about this issue and talking it over with leaders I respect, I think it boils down to one word: mission."

"I know that having a mission is important."

"That's where you're wrong. Mission is not just important, it's vital. Having a mission that challenges and pushes you is the key ingredient to growth in any organization. It is just as vital in the life of the leader as well. Can you clearly communicate to me what your mission is in life and in ministry?" Jerry asked, his eyes looking hard at Truman.

"Well, I guess I have a rough idea. You know, love God and serve Him, love my wife, work with students. Beyond that I can't really put my finger on it."

Jerry picked up his fishing rod. It was already rigged up with a reel, line, bobber, sinker, and hook. He motioned with it to Truman and asked, "What do you think is the most important component of this fishing equipment?"

"I don't know, seems like is all pretty important."

"True," Jerry said. "But I would say that the hook is the critical piece. Without the hook you cannot catch the fish. The hook is the smallest, but most important part. Mission is a lot like that. Your mission in life will encompass many things including your passion, strengths, and desires. But you need to define your mission in a mission statement that functions like this hook here. It should be a short statement that encompasses what it is that you think God wants you to do with your life. Once you have done this for yourself, you can learn how to do it for your ministry."

Jerry grabbed the bait bucket and baited his hook. Truman took his cue from the older man. Once they had cast their lines and were watching their bobbers, Jerry continued, "Your mission can be nailed down by looking at three important ingredients: burden, passion, and vision."

"That sounds simple enough, but I'm going to need you to define those terms," Truman said with a wry smile.

"OK, let's start with burden. Burden can be best described as what breaks your heart. It's when you see a story on the news and you just can't get it out of your mind. Really, your burden is the injustice or cause that you most desperately want to change. So Truman, what cause are you burdened by?" Jerry asked.

"I think I am most sensitive to hurting people," Truman responded.

"Good, but let's make that more specific. What specific group of hurting people do you find yourself drawn to?"

Truman thought for a moment as he looked at the calm waters of the lake. "If you pressed me, I guess I would have to say lost students. I was saved when I was in high school and it was my youth pastor that brought me to the Lord. He helped me learn how to deal with many of the hurts that were in my life."

"That makes a lot of sense. Often we are burdened by things that are close to our personal experience. Now, let's talk about passion. Passion is defined as the things that you love doing. It is what brings you the most joy in life. You know the feeling when you are in your sweet spot and you think that you have made God smile? That's your passion."

"I know just what you mean. I really enjoy being creative. I especially love being creative when it comes to ministry. I also love it when I can help someone who is hurting. Being more specific," Truman smiled toward Jerry, "I am passionate about being creative in ministry so that I can reach and help hurting students."

"Excellent. You are getting the hang of it," Jerry said as he cast his line out in a new spot. "Well, even if the fish aren't biting, you are making progress on your mission statement. Alright, the last step is to identify your vision. Vision is best described as your unique perspective on God's Kingdom. It's what you can see yourself doing to live out your passions and make a difference in your burdens. Any ideas?"

"That's a little harder. I know that it has changed for me over the years as I have gotten to know my abilities and passions better. I guess I would have to say that I see myself finding creative ways to reach out to hurting students, both students who already know God and those who aren't believers yet. Is that specific enough?" Truman asked with a hint of playful sarcasm.

"Sure, that's definitely a good start," responded Jerry. "This step is often the hardest one because, like you said, it can change the most. Often our burdens and passions stay fairly consistent. But our vision can easily change as our perspective on ourselves and God's Kingdom grows and changes."

"So, how can I get a better picture of what my vision might be?" asked Truman.

"The best way to discover your vision is to spend time in communion with God. I believe that vision comes from God and we discover it as we get to know God better. It takes discipline to pray and seek God's will for our lives. As we pray, God will uncover our vision for us. Does that make sense?"

"Yeah, I think I get it. I need to pray and seek God for my vision."
Jerry continued, "Now that we are on a roll, let's take it home. You need to come up with a

mission statement that encompasses all three aspects of mission. You want to make it short and memorable too. What do you think your mission statement could be?"

"Hmmm. Well, I think that it would have to include my burden for hurting students, my passion for creativity in ministry, and my vision for using my current position as a youth worker to affect change in students and the Kingdom. Maybe, it could be 'creatively reaching out to hurting kids at First Community and beyond,'" Truman said triumphantly.

"I like it. Easy to remember and inspiring. I would encourage you to put that up in your office and memorize it. Remember, the thing about mission is that it keeps you on track, keeps your efforts focused on the areas where you will make the most difference. Truly, this mission statement will help you in ways you can't even see yet."

"OK, I think I get it. But how do I translate this into my ministry as a whole?"

"What you need to do is get your most influential leaders together — students, volunteers, and parents — and ask them to go through this same process with you. Have them define the burden, passion, and vision for the ministry. It might take a while as you debate the purpose of your church's youth ministry, but the end result will provide unity and clarity as your team pushes forward. Doing this together will create ownership as well," said Jerry.

Just as Jerry was finishing his thought, Truman watched his bobber dive below the surface of the water. He reared back with his fishing rod and set the hook on a nice largemouth bass of about two pounds. The fish jumped out of the water in an effort to throw the hook. In spite of himself, Truman let out a yell. As he brought the fish to the boat he said to Jerry, "This is the first fish I have caught in years. I forgot how fun this can be." Truman landed the fish, removed the hook, and watched as it disappeared back into the depths of the lake.

"Remember, Truman, just like fishing, life is supposed to be fun. Don't forget that you can enjoy ministry when you are doing it for the right reasons and with the right perspective. Let's see if we can get a bigger one," Jerry said with a grin.

After that their conversation and attention focused on the fishing. The time together did wonders for Truman's soul and cemented the bond that had been growing between the two men. As they approached the dock they promised each other to do this again soon.

Truman drove home with the setting sun. He was more relaxed and satisfied than he had been in a long time. He now understood what he needed to do as a leader, both in his personal life and in his ministry. As he reflected on the time that he had spent with Jerry over the past six weeks, he realized the gift that his wise friend had given him. Leadership no longer was a mystery that eluded him. Jerry had helped him develop the skills he needed to be a successful youth pastor at First Community Church. He was excited and motivated to see where God would take him in the future. He knew his exciting journey had only just begun.

Leadership Principle:
Focusing on Mission: Burden + Passion + Vision = Mission

Effective leaders know their purpose, their mission, and they stay focused on that mission. Leaders will always face competing pressures, and it's easy to get sidetracked. But a clear understanding of mission will keep leaders focused and on task. When they remain focused on their mission, these leaders are able to accomplish so much more because they have kept their eyes on their primary purpose.

The key to any mission is the ability of the leader to be able to communicate it effectively. A mission statement is an easy way to keep the purpose of any organization or group in front of the team members. Mission statements work just as well on a personal level. Knowing your own mission statement as a leader will help you make good decisions about your future and allow you to stay focused on what's important to you.

LeaderTreks uses the time-tested mission statement equation of Burden + Passion + Vision = Mission. Burden is best defined by those issues that really affect you, the things that break your heart. Passion is what you love to do, the things you want to do all the time. Vision is the role you can see yourself playing in God's Kingdom. Taking these three things together gives you a good idea of your mission or purpose as a leader. Boiling it down to a short statement allows your mission to be memorable and central to all that you do as a leader.

Jesus understood His mission and purpose. His mission came directly from his Father and impacted every action of His life. We can see Jesus living out His mission in the way He interacted with the lost and destitute as well as His confrontations with the "religious" beliefs of His time. Look at the following passages and answer these questions about Jesus' mission:

Read: John 10:10, John 4:34, Matthew 9:12-13

If you had to describe Jesus' mission to someone who didn't know Him, what adjectives would you use?

_____

_____

_____

_____

How did Jesus' mission, stated in these passages, affect the way He lived His life?

_____

_____

_____

_____

How is your life's purpose similar to that of Jesus? What are the differences?

_____

_____

_____

_____

What can you learn from Jesus' mission that you can apply to your own life?

_____

_____

_____

_____

Leadership Experience
The LeaderTreks Mission Blueprint

If someone asked you, how would you answer the question, "What is your purpose as a leader?" Many of us would be able to give a vague answer based on how we feel at the moment or what we are working on at the time. The following exercise is designed to help you pinpoint your personal leadership mission. The process can also be extremely helpful for a group or organization that needs to narrow its focus or become unified behind a common mission.

LeaderTreks

Mission Blueprint

STEP 1 – Identify your burden

What causes or issues do you care most about?

_____

_____

_____

If you have free time to volunteer to a charity, where would you volunteer?

_____

_____

When you read the newspaper or watch the news on TV, what news stories most catch your attention?

_____

_____

Define your burden specifically by describing who you are burdened by, what about them burdens you, and what you would want to see done about the problem.

_____

_____

_____

STEP 2 – Name your passion

What are the 1-3 activities that you would do to the exclusion of almost anything else?

_____

_____

_____

When you are happiest and feeling most fulfilled, what do you find yourself doing?

_____

_____

_____

What activities could you do forever? What never gets old for you?

_____

_____

Make a list of the things that you are most passionate about.

_____

_____

STEP 3 – Uncover your vision

What things are most important for you to accomplish in life?

_____

_____

What specific role can you play in God's kingdom?

_____

_____

What might be your niche?

_____

_____

Write out your vision as specifically as you can.

_____

_____

_____

STEP 4 – Create a mission statement

Read over your answers to the first three steps. Note any common themes.

_____

_____

_____

Write out a statement that encompasses all three steps. Don't worry about length at first.

_____

_____

_____

_____

_____

Now, try to shorten your statement to something memorable and concise. This will be your mission statement.

_____

_____

_____

Application

Defining your mission as a leader or clarifying the purpose of your organization is just the first step. Many make the mistake of thinking a mission statement is an end result. The next step is to live this mission out each and every day. Be sure to take your mission statement to the next level by thinking about these questions.

What is one thing that you can do differently tomorrow that will allow you to more fully live out your mission?

_____

_____

_____

_____

How can you bring more of a sense of purpose to your ministry this week?

_____

_____

_____

_____

What can you do to stay true to your mission in the future?

_____

_____

_____

_____

Conclusion

Thanks for taking this leadership journey with us. Our hope is that you have found insight and encouragement from these pages. There is much to learn about leadership. This book represents just a small part of what it takes to be a successful leader.

To get the most out of this book, be sure to review the lessons in a few weeks or months. Give yourself time to learn and apply what you have read here. The crucible of real world leadership will teach you more than any book ever could. By examining the leadership experiences that you already have, you will be able to discover truth in a whole new way. Consider starting a leadership journal to chronicle your progress. As a leader we grow much like a tree—slowly, almost imperceptibly. By journaling about your leadership experiences you will be able to look back over the months and years of your leadership journey and be able to see how you have grown.

Another great leadership habit to adopt from the reading of this book is to find a mentor and to actively mentor other young leaders. Just as Truman had much to learn from Jerry, so too do you have much to learn from older and wiser leaders. Often we are hesitant to approach a leader we respect and ask for mentoring. We don't want to impose on them or force them into something. In reality, those who approach mentors seldom find resistance. Just as you would be honored if someone asked you to mentor them, other leaders see it as an honor to be asked. Prayerfully consider those in your life who can teach you new things about leadership. Make a plan to approach them this week. If you can't think of another leader who could help you in this way, start praying about it. As you pray about it, God will open your eyes or introduce you to someone from whom you can learn. In the same vein, consider finding a young leader you can mentor—maybe a student who graduated from the youth ministry or a volunteer. When you invest in young leaders, you invest in the Kingdom of God.

At LeaderTreks we are constantly thinking of new ways to grow leaders for God's work. We want to be your partner in the process of developing yourself and the other leaders around you. Please check out our website to see all the resources we offer for youth workers, volunteers, and students: www.leadertreks.com   If ever we can serve you, please contact us.

Partnering with youth workers to develop students into leaders.

It's our belief that the church is one generation away from a leadership void and if we don't intentionally develop leaders, the church will struggle. To that end, we developed the LeaderTreks model for leadership development. We apply this model to all the resources and training events we offer.

LeaderTreks comes along side of youth workers providing:

• Leadership training events for students

• Leadership resources

• Leadership driven mission and wilderness trips

• Youth Worker Training

Check out our website at www.leadertreks.com

877-502-0699

Developing Leaders to Fulfill the Great Commission